I0796716

Behind the State Capitol: Or Cincinnati Pike

John Wieners

50th Anniversary Edition

Edited by Raymond Foye with new essays
by Robert Dewhurst and James Dunn

The Song Cave

ASPHODEL, In Hell's Des
The JUDSON POETS' THEATER
Rt 3 Box:
Lana Turner
(America's former
"sweater girl")
LETT
Januar
Mr. Jol
44 Joy
Apt. 1
Boston
Thank
Dear M
heartw
do my
seated
sped th
and ho
of love
places,
noon,

A collection of poetry, written by John Wieners in The United States.

BEHIND THE STATE CAPITOL: OR CINCINNATI PIKE

Cinema decoupages; verses, abbreviated prose insights.

The Good Gay Poets

This collection is in response to earlier requests from the hands of Allen Ginsberg, who was responsible for securing the success of my first international volume; to Tom Maschler for correspondence in pertinence over that forgoing compilation from contracted Author, Suite Ten, Forty Four Joy Street, Boston, Massachusetts. 723U S A8376

ISBN 0-915480-00-X
LC 75-6121

CONTENTS

1952

Beyond this river which I have no desire to cross
There are mountains which I have no desire to climb
I am fenced in by rivers and mountains
And though year's day goes, I feel no loss.

Where am I that I am forced to stay?
Why wake to life that holds no hopeful dawn?
What have I lost that all these losses matter not?
You do not answer World, you cannot say!

They have taken from you also, all the best
And leave you with your speech and sight a sham.
Yes, you can speak and see but there is nothing left
To stare and stutter over with the rest

Why, why is it so, since there is nothing here
We force ourselves to wait and watch our life
Empty of peace and empty of love.
Remembering always remembered the former faithful year!

UNDERSTOOD DISBELIEF IN PAGANISM, LIES AND HERESY

Prick any literay dichotomy
sung unrent gibberish from maxim skulls
west Manchester cemetery

recidivist testimony damned
promulgated post-mortem Harry Ghouls
wills pleasant chicanery hulled

in opposition to queer honesty,
flying hapless good humours
Morphe erroneous untedious mystery,

non-said mistakes; pure levity
to a method of confused doubt;
lipping erratic contrary indexd

Brevity; yes or no arsinine Coliseum
arrogance, attrib. Constant shout
Emperor Hippocratic misaligned

green breviary Ursuline stiff codecil.
A prayerbook, black Catholic mint
bogus mendicants Parsifal muff

Taught in the text as poor flopped sisters,
reeked convent blood between pleas
of gospel purblind drawn melodramas.

Silk-ribbon circus twined, border rhyme.
Povertystricken grandfathers hymnal
Less-allowed than San de Remo cape civil

War Reolutionary caval.
House Father across Sunday common roof
"But they're all ivoried brooch (navel

running marines the other way."
Spies vision for impertinently, drugs
when you're awake.

A viscosity submandered elopes
deluge senseless colophon
Forgotten opposition

in the face of negligent monetary
station or bookstore adherent nation.
(Debauched, bequeathed goad.)

SIGNS OF THE PRESIDENT MACHINE

I've got 25¢ coin on the bureau
or maple mahoganny table, built out of
magnolia limbs, and a persian carpet airing in lawn

yard a baby flood, TELVA magazines with my photograph on
the cover as Mariln Monroe, jack dead mother's nutty sister
saying, *Who Is She*, I'm A Lot of Man, by the late Nancy
    Cunard, of course

that pauvre Rose La Rose, Billie Shakespeare, or was it Sanctity's
                                        Holiday drugged as Moynihan across
behind a red lantern, ask Mme Brenda drinking torpid Gloucester
        cyan-
ide dutied United States Postmen, plastic transparent basket.

Poor Benedict posing as a Polish sister
I can feel his dope over the Hedges, wintergardening carol from
the Meirovingian corner besides
the master bedroom, the military treason in their acquisition
from accumulation in the United Feds prison of
not only food at Agriculture, but terms of language, love and
fashion.

Pussybile, fresh from black George's suicide at 86 Charles.

Oh, yes, a week of, a month of, two years moving shirts with
Treasury numbers
poor secretaries becoming international thieves, from failure
to absorb
newly hung curtains, encroaching plants and poisoned burners
on the stove coiled charcoal sexual yens in the dish dryer.

NOT THIS AGONY OF LOVE, WITHOUT BEING LOVED

Not this agony in the process of life
to wake up and find
you love, while he cannot

another does cherish your self in *like* way
you idolize his ecstasy
maintained as a hot kiss

upon my neck. Oh this in an
exercise, trained by sentiment, sinews

sentience, surrender, sweet sundered sleep.
Keep the tryst, trust further
to his mind's vision, where against

travel, time, ruesome new companions it may
be contained for the terrain we must encounter and surmount.

Substance, non, a glad awakening
a quick trip, trick long preserved
for the distance on his book, named.

Cross country, we would not be betrayed
by the art of goodness, lust, our bodies
tell poetry, spirits his wife speaks of
in the singular, sometimes.

Equally, likewise, there is a dependence
for generosity, upon his mother, a woman
in whose beauty, there reigneth my

hope, standard.

FETE VERSES FROM FEARFUL RESURRECTIONS

When I think stand
of out crowd I cut bleeding at my finger tips
only I was too ill
to enjoy singlely them,

and they were to stretch harridan point,
professionally committed bug,
not to belabor either fact
in self construed wishfully

stars on Hunter boards at Juilliard's
a mere decade or 2 between
Nedicks & Jack 54th St. Playhouse
quikstick buses enroute stage-place;

O'h did get assaulted with stranger's gun,
Easter Bet' hopelessly run over by limousine,
who jumped off Ariad's roof,
and fatedly LBC estranged.

TO SINK LOVE

Are you up late this evening
to another man
do I miss you in the empty bed across the room
I was waiting for you to get up here.

That's to a third person
Gratification around the clock
desperate Netherlands destiny
when feelings within my bones body cry

out as before by massive embrace to be held
I beg I bring you closer
with each word I write/I hope
your loveliness, despite jealousy
plays beauty upon my head
upon your breast. I exist

for your kiss. The poets' paradise
expells in tune latencied disservice
modishly spelld, a dream dispelled
after yesteryear cinema

Can you see, I have forgotten or
am not qualified to shoulder when want
should become our man of god's purpose,
to perpetuate my person, peaked at that passion
where I have lost my way, my reason for even debating
question.

JAIL MATA HARI?

for Alan Davies

Mata Hari was three women un
questiond . And her name wasn't faith,
hope or charity. Nor a good neighbor policy toward virtue.

An heart past breast caution blossom
in memory's calm taxd ration strength
a semi-incapacitated glace cort diadem.

Maud trinket; mere bauble under cool
ventd calm collect as lieu propulsion
she perpetrates for me this stronghold

of a nation's Knox reservoir, where blood
begat treasond request over telephone info-
rmation their airborne's squadron mood

discloses identity baby morgue, end. I am thy charlatan
post notice daily via curtaind scarcity
the salute solidizes assault out detainment.

An evening's liberty; twenty year gushing broad
encompassement Ithaca; Corning wraith
vinyl oil prypeller sin. lubricates heinous legend.

Travelling her own speed; no adduction she enchanted
audiences after thirty 8 leagues *bouttonniere*
malice toward none; her secret forgiving pardon.

Suppose murder less done; the terrible winter snows gatherd
avalanche length to bombard swathes canyons of cities
she owned outright; night after night as Venus play bed

horsepowerd to outfox tyrannized legions rippd forment
she could suspend cement, as untendd captains breakwater
a mazebad sabotage a whodone-it weaponless garment.

As receiptd, intrigue scandal. These her diet, venom
labor crews, mores wittingly deal in call accusation.
Preaching vestements at sundown like purpose path.

Could she see ink dial; task as sorceress sans citadel?
Honesty sirens enmeshed appeal entertrip submits
interrogation, I outlast treachery, outmanoeuver titles.

Outshine parsimony; matrimony my goal; alas entaild youth.

TOADY'S SINGULAR

for Gerard Malanga

No wonder non-congregated as faded weather they can write good poems,
They're in hell for doing it; Mafia currency minter.

They try to stop morning wind blowing on Afro-american vain prayerleaf
cursed passport-less academics, as unattempted one they despised.

No swans, pregnant Amalfi conducive-like May Tuesday
Nor you, impeccable blond man, in dagger cloak bearded crossing custom gate inspection.

On Morrocan citadel plural spires Northerm minarets roost for aviary nest
printing deliveranced keep futuristic ominous words of ghoulish Sunday sermon warning

For our more future, as parched imbecilic Mata Hari, beloved up
To barefoot high chieftains of Salerno, not cobblestone dob-individual

genied istortes, 123. Stares burning naive police lamps public-Garden

Chicago correspondent deprived connect hour

This hapless, high heeled arch-ingenue foe of waned arsinine
Impecuniousness, posing our liberators in to Prussian Piepel.

Ion Charles stoop

MA'S DECK CHAIRS

Just that permission
this morning
after lunch, an open window
to see those old, masculine things
in this big house, the empty
bathroom, when bachelor means
leisure to read kitchen curtains --
her earings upon plate at Stearns, R.H.
harvest sheaf lamps from Chicago, Murano ashtray back Dahl's
Geary in Frisco, with nearly 2 carats of stone
notupstairthe Bullocks, Burdines pot & pillow.

Made lunchdate at Mayfair, what could you buy?
Suite facing Pacific Life-Los Angeles clip cloche
merely socks White House to certify Lords
Churchill & Chesterfield patent
"one perception must directly lead
to another!

UPON MATA HARI PAUL MALL

With a daring green frequent money bankroll
for Turkish adventuresses A.W.O.L. minus bail
albeit 19th Infant Saviour from Hanover grand toll

wards back and forth, suing Moritat dawn patrol
less permission from the mercenary recoil baccarat jail
covers soil aspersion of southern trench turmoil:

too bad a covey useless birds of prey empty sale.
Their out foreign correspondence Czechs Olympic details
history lose one, win one as two obvious literary trial

overplowed a concert hall crisis in swooping terms rogue pale
serving sacrifice crossing customs anticipating mail.

"HOW DARE YOU?

These winter clothes
choke the untried throat
between hands friendless
or definite, darksome streets

    Without money,
what can one do but
respond to their calls
& preen fetishly

at deepend of bar stools
in scarlet rooms where Spicer hangs
still on Wurlitzer nooses
blitzkreiger sexy moons &

an old hand between your legs.

    Two on a match, after
thoughts of fame & the future
travelling Sunday glibly Golden gate
15 years ago, Columbus & Stockton

the Fillmore clan nightime mansions, --
what's this crust
after addicts refuse to recognize calendars?
Meeting the same diners over & over again
at the beach, in the bar.

DOM PERIGNON

1959

One of us is going to die,
I dont know which
champagne and cake on the balcony
geraniums newly planted after the rain,
dogs baying to the moon.
The geraniums,
their faces freshly painted
flow/in the moon, also of the wall
with a luminous red I have never seen before --
at twilight --
the sky grey
but the geraniums
vibrous
different than the firefly
different than the contralto
singing
Schubert's Last Songs,
four of them
different from the Bavarian Gentians
of Lawrence.
Only you, geraniums alone
of the moon.

Unpublished Composition Dennison Road, Summer Annisquam,

1966

HANGING ON FOR DEAR LIFE

Charles Olson has not for me since his death, become a colossal bore And I thought that's what happened to most dead practicers of verse-composition by FIELD or open formalization poets. I have written so much about him, in the fifteen years or so mindless, give one or more -- like two, I met him and that's all I can say, is to go read his works. Or the poems. Or the men who practiced him, or those who wrote for him, or for whom he wrote. Gerard Malanga, Robert Creeley, Robert Duncan, Vincent Ferrini, Gerrit Lansing, Joel Oppenheimer and Robert Kelley, including myself, and countless others, William Carlos Williams, Edward Dahlberg, Jonathan Williams and Dorothy Norman.

Nobody can say a nicer thing than if it's like going to Miami for the National Democratic Convention this year from Boston by car, three days to get there, three days to get back, two days down there! but if one had never been to Miami before it's worth the trip. Charles Olson is worth the trip. Leroi Jones is as well as Ed Dorn, men highly influenced by Mr. Olson's figure, outward.

Without a social stigma, or and by that I mean, any form of sexuality, going down by the river at night, whether for pleasure or sightseeing, one of the finest texts Charles mentioned to us at Black Mountain College was "After the Pleasure Party," by Herman Melville; on foot or in car, one thinks of the first place one "met" him at The Charles Street Meeting House when Charles mentioned his navigator's tools or pilot's compass for charting the depths of unfathomed waters, seeing to steer a man straight. I am not going to make the compromise of seeking love on strange shores, just because it's available. it doesn't of necessity follow that available means are the most satisfactory. I have to investigate love or feeling or emotion or romance where it lies at its most familiar. Charles was a familiar person to my mind for 15 years. It doesn't follow that he taught me more than anybody else, including my mother and father. One doesn't expect he should have the qualities of doing about almost everything else. But it is a relief to get away from one's condition and see it the bizarre oddity it actually is to other persons.

Regarding poetry, it isn't always what one says as content in his work, the moon rising over Indian burying grounds, Apollo and the Nine be bliss to the cold of two men on a winter evening, stopped by the police for transporting hot property after three in the morning, to the rising sun that was reflected canary-yellow in his, were they blue, or azure, or hazel eyes?

When I think of the few scanty books in my library, I know that he was the world of literature for me. I fear I drove him out of all sorts of men whom he knew, never playing the hermit or lonely recluse. He kept many marriages going simultaneously on points during endless affairs. Al Cook befriended him at a time when he needed it most. Walter Cohen was always inviting him to dinner, with his wife Bette, who edited *Audit* with Charles Doria, whose translations of *The Sanchuniathon* Professor CO laid in my lap. Ralph Maud came to interview him. Allen Ginsberg honored him always in conversation and attention Capitoline hill and the Forum over on Park Avenue south assimilated and Kenneth Koch entertained him, as Gregory Corso, out in the Boston Hills during a visit from the newspaper publisher from downeast town, Maine's John Grady.

We seldom allow what is beneath our dignity. Pretty low class at the time, rooming above a clothing store and using that summer of 1966 to stay in town, until they sailed for London on the Empress of Canada, harboring Montreal in retrospect for any needyperpendicularity. Having admired Jack Kerouac's *Doktor Sax*, Joe Early and I spent an evening with Olson over in his apartment, but then Malanga started taking the edge on his time. He welcomed all sorts of men, in twenties now he or we seem to have the habit for many things. Supper, cigarettes, leisure, loneliness.

ALIDA VALLI

I am sitting in the presence of Alida Valli, now, the woman who I worshipped for thirty years, as an actress, a real person, and a movie star. A good person who means to me the world.

How I cherished her, and kept her alive in my heart. And wondered what had become of her. From one film to the next. Since *The Miracle of the Bells,* by Russell Janeway, with Fred MacMurray and Frank Sinatra, who I believe you know.

You know since I was a boy, I never knew who was a movie actor, or a stage thespian either.

Alida Valli has retained all her charm, her loveliness and intelligence with *The White Mountain,* a novel by James Ramsay Ullman, opening next to the Paramount she remembers above others that authorship, whose adoration and excellence brightened our youth. And who collected the photographs and newspaper reports of their combined performances in Sir G. Greene's story, *Third Man* with great relish, including *Weep No More*, confined with the late, great Thespian Mister Claud Rains. Then there was The Paradine Family Case, scandalous affair, and the Madrid museum cameo appearance, of a humorous bent.

Alida Valli does not know me, yet she as the guise underploy *Letter From* Ste. Zweig's *Unknown Woman,* inscribed a L. Jordan, addresses still; viz. witness the recent notice, casting her as Shakespeare's focal parentage in an adaption of her son's mistress, Ophelie, at *The Playboy,* nearby the Elspeth, Holman-Reynolds tragedy, portraying erstwhile King of Denmark's mater, Gertrude.

With her total comprehension in decorum and of someone she does know, without a syncopation, I recollect she may care, as she so indicated in Carson City, Nevada, to listen again, with her blatant mention of this chapeaux, purchased in Wm. Filene's and Sons; it takes a great deal of work, three hundred years at least, to learn the diction she has. As Faye Dunaway by The Five-Spot; Alida de Mejo shall receive the few cups of tea, alloted to us, as performers in the United States

At the comrades in town, Boston's community, but we need all the help we can get. What is wrong with Valli, anyway? 10 days and I have been intermittently pondering, earlier my cause for her mind and anatomy to chalk up, as below par. The reason?

Hepatitus, too many writhings owing from child-bearing, world-position pertinently, worst assumption verified. The Hispanic child-rack. A particular punishment, inflicted upon higher primates resulting in deteriotation.

The nature of mal feasance bemuses ruin claiming after heated ambition, needlessly overt, to stunt performance whatever one's goal. It could surface with irascible reaction in politic's manners, shortsighting environment, retention and endowed indubitableness. I've had a cross to bear, for thirty-five years, my mother's cursed bane equally alleged.

Were it not for crucified faith, utterable testament the sweet companionship of her power-house, I'd never have known the tax abroad claimed within aristocracy. Well it's known, to harp upon a crooked bow, gold lame lies irreducible, a shard nervedly restorn. Can Spanish main stay trestle cure diesel Fancy.

Her travel mingles in discrimination. A super-imposed overleaf, in conjunction akin polity, simultaneity for want of better words, stententorian. I could surmise sybaratic aggressor, before post data, a primitive torture rack, or collapse of an honorable estate; caverned fall in; the later stems likely. in a vein of Herucaneum, or Pompei. With a plethora of Gibbons, patrician bans in effect strengthen The Messrs. Late Durgin, Selznick, Hitchcock, Rank 'ideas and opinions.'

You think I'm normal, they do a lot of things to my mind. She mentions her mother, who I was. And her work in Occupation Offices was to be regretted since the neo-fascists obtained money w/o permission from e.g. bloc stalemate Schmidt Ingrid Isabel Fludd, and of course from Yugoslavia, where Ms. Valli was born. Of that, more later.

This money in member nations inauguration issue circulates au compagne. 'What's Hecuba to us, what Bulgaria and what becomes of Bulgaria? who rules in Bulgaria it's all the same to us; the whole question of our friendship with *Occidente . . .'*

A QUESTION

"I didn't ask, just made a stab
in marriage, between two men

Prinz K. may
not wed any,
another
boy, boogy-wig, cream blouse, out
on the stoop
broom clad turnip apr
on speaking, Joe

Early standing finally
of conspires children as probation.
Down south, still a problem.

Two Murphys and a Donleavy
a cross between Tracy and Taylor
piss on in the medicine chest
at our age, abduction between
two males

THE HAND OF THE SCULPTOR

To my Grandmother

Bewildered at times, in public situations, what woman hasn't portrayed, interrogation implied imposition, intimidated *tout le monde* c'est le guerre coquette for protection, as William spouted -- "against the slings and arrows of outrageous fortune," one and often many occasions present themselves sufficiently to the mind for self-rectification in sere-quoted terms, acquitted precautionary measure, resultant against any magnified exaggeration re-occurence.

Pre-meditated e.g. the occasion of snares, from already plausible resurrection taking mathematically into account irrelevant connectives or quoting earlier constructive, ignoble demolitions unremarkably subtract obviously present day confraternity that men in like evident from number amazedly hail surprise, so to say, approximately.

I am glad I mean to know little of either, the confinement unto our weaker species, or the oncrushing avalanche from enemy craft.
Consternation in the realm of reason,
confrontation of the unknown.

scracity through renown
filial devotion.

Oh providence to imagination we add thy blessings unto our own
And commit comradeship from taught arm of His companion.

Evaporated age relief over material needs
a staunch allegiance upon government seats
of capital power accompany attainment

envisioning architecture as foul human reality
to divine evidence without recourse from
temporal conscience in the garb-fare success,

discounted advances thorough congress ploughed sentate.
I give credence to national patriots regardless
semi-personal politics and to neighborly proctors.

Why aren't we good enough to walk the streets? Oblivious

to any origin
erstwhile destinies, oh wrought contourd delineation
proof immured a town well; square hitch miracled ladle
veritably
Haven't we all bathed au naturel under consoled exemplar
to sparkling beds

CONTEMPLATION

Why do they turn away from us
on the streets when we love
them. Billie Holiday was the story
of my whole life & still is

on sunlit Sunday afternoons

opposite the elevated railroad
tracks
at Cambridge street & Charles
when every hope burns to stinking incontinence,

the winter wind blows sand & sea off countless holiday
extravaganzas, between body & soul

Sultry California boulevards proliferate upon a shredded
mortality, as the abyss of former promenades wells

to fecundate interiorly
again at Land's
End.

The pleasures of young escapades envelopes
smoked glass store-fronts outside the empty Scotch & soda
orders.
Bar.

FAREN FERRIES

That's what they have ceiling lights for,
bilge remembered earlier flamed
no matter how many owers timed
Watt riot bonfire bulbs' order

sure temper massacre every man,
under suspicion over fraternal citizen
in rout from his consciend Mohammedan
an easy tent when Turkish snipers foreign

sired hero's mind. Neon kleigs blind *SSiS*
witness Irving Wallace, an *Idol* crew nook
spoken portrait exhibited falcon maltese puke
for case of disaster, bogus DC show carcass.

Float electrified currency city headline,
a mother's memory should ax pier slaughter,
together on 10th Avenue twin Caroline star routine
as good as tomorrow's edition in gold Jenifer.

Who didn't dare aim faster anyone over this kiss,
an abeyance from plural intimate response,
nonetheless shadowy interference shifting our places
has caused likewise chnce changed address.

Somewhat Tennessee Williams' long distance Father Moe
Smyrna turned up fror Laurette Valli's sham,
like the no *Sweet Bird of Youth* losing Acapulco
tan on fun occasion, when his genuine theater warred Ham.

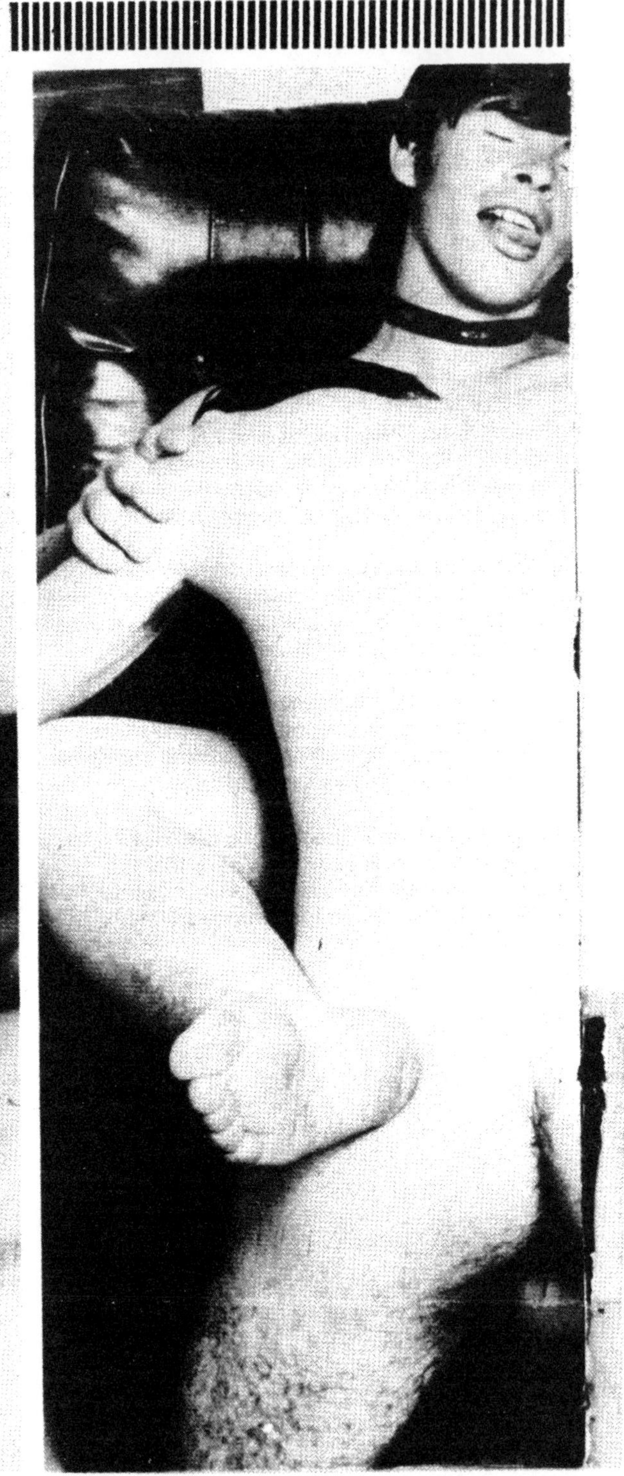

A PUHLS PENCIL BOX

To John Derek or Richard Conte

There are three men I love most in the world; Johnny Stompanato, Benjamin "Bugsy" Seigel and Serge Rubenstein. Not that I need the public approval; simply God removed them from when I as Lana Turner, Virginia Hill and Joan Woodward needed them most. I was no one then. Not even an NE to my name; an unknown struggling to be a New Yorker, a starlet or a dynamite model out of the Immaculate Conception. That was in 1950 when the Russian Nobleman, Serge Rubenstein was shot in his Fifth Avenue apartment, near the Sherry Netherlands, was it where he was so brutally sensationalized. I have read the Biography of His life and wonder who, why and when my visit to the Big City concurred for his extinction. The gangland slaying involves me needlessly in prior obscurity.

The Benjamin Siegel slaying coincided was it to an hostility that ended in the summer of 1965, when the Madam Hill from a supposed overdose of sleeping pills perished outside of Vienna. Wasn't she that evening interwoven to a fabric of novels undertaken through a great serialization of corn, namely approximate loss of year, melodrama and continuity from the 1950's pinups? Benjamin Siegel was well-known in the same world that Serge Rubenstein moved. Their testaments to my efforts as the said Virginia and Joan ally a beneficent tolerance to my fallible, daily grind, errant pursuedly prostrate ajar popularity portals. Not only that, G-men suggest witness moribund legalized bestowal I condition prierairies to the truth that someday it may be both their willingness to serve Her Holy Mother, be accepted and their martyrs punished before the wrongdoers supplied rotten corporeality unto state means.

Could the news-hounds supplement execution by exhumation?

Ben was only a name. Hill may have been it. That's spelled double L, who also dated Prince S.

Fiddle surveillance from Brigham's to Murray's?

Debt to perdited, no matter which way you read, lovy?

John C----- happens to remain with testimony I shall never see, no matter how I am. The gooks, crocks, and dwarfs of Borneo hold no message for mankind, no questions asked out of Penny Cateschism, no needling from abatement indicated forecasts fancily supply their easy consciences, ignorance's expense burns them as pidgeons in the rotogravure tabloids, where mine gets an occasional plug, of a difference's stock to feather your admission. Then who learns permission sustained wisdom. A bold, carless homocide a man and vain woman attains acquired malevolence from thousands in retaliation.

Having money to punish murderers of men shot down bec because they loved, as those girls without any skill in knowing it. Working out of penny grocery or drug stores at soda fountains, bread lines and cereal boxes, towelling away earned hours before the beaming showers from benzedrine or hop-head wolfbane but earnest to plan ahead and save pennies for althe-letic sweaters, jersey hairtoniques and mind-dark glasses, as broad as smirk predicted to my future, your dead small capital alive. T' make no mistake about it, self relinquished corpse Admittedly eternal stay these with out of the pure passionate throbbing of their hearts, sewn up into my thighs, for the million-dollar marquees.

I trust the Lower East-Side and was a friend of well-dressed informants, bulwarked good natures of writers, before world working stolidty's famine. He was my father, they say he came from Hell's Kitchen and was a friend of George Plympton and one of the Valentine's Day assailants; keeping his nose clean for our sake. Yet something possessed him, after we went to bed, to do us in. I couldn't tell you why. It was just one of those things. On the sunny side of the street, across the gulf of the inebriate and impervious.

He dressed well, they said and did I not like it, lose his hair to drinkers and lushes. Forgive me but VA always stands up to an inebriate; if that's what Ben forgot, only the Austrian immigration laws allow restitution to what he released as his behind.

Ay, bill it all to the Washington Post, the New York Post, the Boston Post, you like them most.

Coming for dinner, John dapper smart, tan and polished spic span, in same company, Fay Colony only could love him so. She of most starched propriety, blazoning before west Park ministerial as an heroine before each socialite solly to smote their penances. When occurenace Greenwich, La Jolla or Sydney loosed marine in *The Proud and Profane*, or ship's mariner in GD street, unto fashion reporter for RB as penultimate goal. South of Los Angeles lies San Diego, south of Diego lies Tia Juana, south Tia lies Rocky smeared in cliffs San Juana blue and white scary to assess the death throttling in those voids, these cataclysms off the AF the marrooned catastrophes wraith remain. Not almond as there in Mexico's baseless relatives no good toremember purgatory swore to cherish.The swell tie, casual rhumba, a complete works coalish diamond tacks, as I declare to envision, TNT siren.

With that to recompense, any teenage murderer telepathic long distances swanky peruke off Richard's Arabian Nights. Marmeduke to more swell lotus lanes before Jeanne said pepe-nous, proximate as General Piedmont UN wound for decipherment, taciturn modiste. I contained many balls within my brains as youth grew, exteriorly receptive a puzzle long absences, casually surprised release to segment hero-worship from godly continence. Diddling several infatuations, incognizant any pattern so naive as that cult of chastity, suppressed deeper than seamy Russian, and often dangerous pawn roulette. As any master knew, I could not but surmise the West. Scoffing paintings, timorous to self indulging artists and intimidated musically, dancing aroused sensual raptures leading to zany protestations, largely layered guilt.

Trust funds have no heirs. Where surmounts that dish-out tears steppean corsages. His marble Fifth Ave. front door, languid floral Lenten double decker to marr the climax of NATO in velvet lapels and aortal singed Dover of megaliths less a Black seraglio for continuing to blossom every hour without fail. Bless the burly sweet New York Madison low brows inundation preview Kush if hansom or hacks toll then why won't men lost consciously in discussion wish they knew some peasant at present in fortune.

EliW terminals of Las Vegas prose in poetry, dale's stuccos like Beverly Hills or duplex palace Centro, "donnez-moi Monsieur register", scanned skimmed a relatively old scandal, *The National Examiner,* April 5th, 1958, in proximity the Cranes were implicated for no apparent reason as homocides in their mother's home. My darlings but no one. Even as a little boy hurt a paramour to the Mattapan, as far as I know. Or at the Oriental, either. Both of them paramount desire to bring men closer. And women, made for each other their foolish hearts. You see a girl going alone into the movie house? She's always in trouble in the afternoon.

They think that interests me, it doesn't. In the 40 years that I have been witness.

In relation to a dissolution of daily newspaper, mastheaded
JOHN Fox

FROM MS' KAY KELLY'S SATURDAY REVIEW PRESS
The Wonderful World of Women's Wear Daily, **1972.**

Bergler called "a clinical psychiatric-psychoanalytic method." When the whole thing was over, Bergler came to one conclusion: "The majority of the really creative persons in the field are male homosexuals." Bergler wrote: "It has never been publicly acknowledged that the majority of the great male fashion creators and hairstylists, both foreign and domestic, are homosexuals. But it has been whispered for decades." As far as Bergler was concerned, "The homosexual's commanding position in the fashion field is a fact." The end. So be it. Love it or leave it.

POPULAR LIBRARY
Her Cold Love Set Men Aflame
My FORBIDDEN PAST
(CARRIAGE ENTRANCE)
The RKO motion picture starring Robert Mitchum, Ava Gardner and Melvyn Douglas is based on this book
MY FORBIDDEN PAST

THE MURDER OF CHEAP WAITRESSES

From Ellen Needham, indicted for their slaying
to Alan Myronwitz' interdit we got to clean up poor classes
"Kill them off", as his unproduced revue, "Shoot the President"
barely two decades late, with Uncle Eddie's "Oh, Oh" was he
Earl Warren
then? we got nothing to say this morning, after returning
from New York.

When the Maid of Mistd Orleans vacationd off The Y in
Room 517, with Charlie
at the wheel, both ways
under
orange lights, does an initial replace a proper name, does a Judge
ressurrect codes, can Anna
'h live, Elizabeth Short, will Cyril join John give orders, or take
them.

The death of hard-working women allowing some a cup of
coffee surprises us, that their slayings
pass unnotc-
ied, yes the fields of Brewster, Willimantic embankments,
now Buddy,
no more Treason in the
telephoneless rooms, on the Eighth Street billboard display.

DO YOU KNOW WHAT CORPSES SAY

I have always loved Clare Trevor, especially this rainy Tuesday,
during the two-day art house revival perigrenate her tough
gun-moll
face in the lobby, as she stood looking

next door garden, for chic fan club reception

Clare, little sister to Saint Francis,
has the Commonwealth black & white mugging
traumatized your Monday *Enquirer?*

attention, and shall
you return Maria; in the balcony last night
we alone sat Jack Benny before your re-enactment in

shining armor, too late healed their slothful wounds.

Go on revolutionized Clare, relive your 2nd World War
memories, be the underworld call girl, his heiress
tryannized+after dark in bed, our Army nurse

And Saloon Madam Song Bird Tahoe

HIATUS

Rest in the dream, that's all I can do.
Hear bells tinkle on the grass
and birds sing.

Smoke in bed
wait for your return
all morning long.

Sit on silken pillows
worked with peacock designs
and golden swans.

Write poems
before a yellow table
in the dawn all morning long.

See Mrs. Coyle the landlady
eat milkweed drunkenly
then do three days' dishes
in the sink all morning long.

Watch her pass before the dragon lilies,
lock the foundry shed,
each single event invested with divinity,
then the pause
when no words come
for the rest of the morning.

HONG KONG BOASTS A HOTEL FOR DEAD

To Massachusetts General Hospital
0913896 - 07 28 74

"Nestled among the steel and glass skyscrapers of Modern Hong Kong sits an unusual hotel — all of its residents are dead!
For many Chinese, the place of burial is very important.
So while their relative waits to ship their remains back to their birthplace in China or to bury them in a burial spot with good 'fung shui' (luck), the Tung Wash Coffin Home serves as a temporary resting place.
The Tung Wash is run on the same principles as a hotel for the living. Rates are fixed and bodies receive regular attention and for those whose relatives cannot pay the rent, there is a proper procedure of eviction -- burial!
Unlike most hotels the rooms are not numbered. Instead each room is given a name such as 'Longevity Room' or 'Room of Quietude.' In one of the refrigerator-like high ceilinged rooms lay the remains of the hotels oldest guests: Madame Tang, who has been there since December 13, 1906, and her husband Tang Kam-Chi, who joined her 9 years later. But not all of the bodies have private rooms, some rest in a far more communal setting. For example, in the biggest hall, the Sun Moon Hall, are rows and rows of paper-wrapped coffins of all sizes, shapes, makes and ages perched on wooden stools. Nearby, tin-boxed skeletons exhumed after 7 years burial in Government cemeteries rest peacefully on iron racks."

POST - MATIN

Haunts post
ast indecipherable
acquisition a baby

Steinway Key in company
Horsey balmy belfry

fastly wraithd

Those are the boys
I think have been over-ridden

Not that guy in the state house

non Globe theatre, that's a

big bring-down
cramming big part.

A NEW BENEFIT

Mints informer
by permanent comparison
unallowed good rebuttal

I'm almost dropped to
my seat, honest

injun.
shoddy interiors dis
avowed

props & opening
nite bouquets

restored

rented in New Jersey.

Anecdote

After several years of having her in their midst, the locals find Mrs. Onassis tame news indeed. They are inclined to ignore her, which she likes.

Only one anecdote has ever circulated about the famous renter. It seems the Casey farmhouse has a French fence around it, a fence of narrowly woven stakes.

Jackie telephoned her landlords and said she'd like to take the fence down. She said her husband, who is rather short and stocky, couldn't see over it, and she wanted Ari to be able to enjoy the view of the neighboring town and hills.

The Caseys refused the request, but did send over a workman who cut a panel out of the fence and put it on hinges.

Now, when in residence, the panel can be lifted. And Aristotle Onassis, that wily world traveler and cosmopolite, a Greek born in Turkey with Argentinian citizenship, a man reputed to be worth one thousand million dollars, can sit and admire the view of Peapack, New Jersey!

Around the environs of the Essex Hunt there are some ambivalent ideas expressed about Jackie Onassis which echo the kind of "yes, she is" — "no, she isn't" opinions often heard around international salons.

There are those who admire Jackie's down-to-earth approach to her bucolic weekend life out of Manhattan, her desire for privacy, and her hope to get away from it all and back to nature.

But there are also those who accuse her of always wanting it both ways for herself.

These are the "does she

'Jackie wanted a fence taken down so that Ari could enjoy the view'

FOR WHAT TIME SLAYS

Scheduled *Summer 1962*

The fog flung over the fields.

The dew heavy on the individual stalks of grass
or weed. The beetles making just the right sound
in the woods, and on the top of the highest tree,
a bird cackling.
The smell of green weeds on the pathway. Whitman's
poems to MANHATTAN, "Give me the splendid silent
sun" all the crowds now dead.
And in the day I am tormented by the memory of
warm supper clubs at night, never crowded, the
way a young man opens the door,
        Mambah singing therè, as Mabel Mercer, on a
                kitchen chair.
         For I have looked down into the pit and turned
        away trembling.

C H I L DREN OF THE WORKING CLASS

to Somes

from incarceration, Taunton State Hospital, 1972

gaunt, ugly deformed

broken from the womb, and horribly shriven
at the labor of their forefathers, if you check back

scout around grey before actual time
their sordid brains don't work right,
pinched men emaciated, piling up railroad ties and highway
ditches
blanched women, swollen and crudely numb
ered before the dark of dawn

scuttling by candlelight, one not to touch, that is, a signal panic
thick peasants after *the* attitude

at that time of their century, bleak and centrifugal
they carry about them, tough disciplines of copper Inidanheads.

there are worse, whom you may never see, non-crucial around
the
spoke, these you do, seldom
locked in Taunton State Hospital and other peon work farms
drudge from morning until night, abandoned within destitute
crevices odd clothes
intent on performing some particular task long has been far
removed
there is no hope, they locked-in key's; housed of course

and there fed, poorly
off sooted, plastic dishes, soiled grimy silver knives and forks,
stamped Department of Mental Health spoons
but the unshrinkable duties of any society
produces its ill-kempt, ignorant and sore idiosyncracies.

There has never been a man yet, whom no matter how wise
can explain how a god, so beautiful he can create
the graces of formal gardens, the exquisite twilight sunsets
in splendor of elegant toolsmiths, still can yield the horror of

dwarfs, who cannot stand up straight with crushed skulls,
diseases on their legs and feet unshaven faces and women,
worn humped backs, deformed necks, hare lips, obese arms

distended rumps, there is not a flame shoots out could ex-
tinguish the torch of any liberty's state infection.

1907, My Mother was born, I am witness t-
o the exasperation of gallant human beings at g-
od, priestly fathers and Her Highness, Holy Mother the Church
persons who felt they were never given a chance, had n-
o luck and were flayed at suffering.

They produced children with phobias, manias and depression,
they cared little for their own metier, and kept watch upon
others, some chance to get ahead

Yes life was hard for them, much more had than for any blo
ated millionaire, who still lives on
their hard-earned monies. I feel I shall
have to be punished for writing this,
that the omniscient god is the rich one,
cared little for looks, less for Art,
still kept weekly films close for the
free dishes and scandal hot. Some how
though got cheated in health and upon
hearth. I am one of them. I am witness
not to Whitman's vision, but instead the
poorhouses, the mad city asylums and re-
lief worklines. Yes, I am witness not to
God's goodness, but his better or less scorn.

The First of May, The Commonwealth of State Massachusetts,
1972.

BY THE BARS

Oh, now, my own poor, good Mother, do not make me ill now.

As four pidgeons walk saucily on the road
and this pen chases them off
with a great flap of wings
before an auto comes along the yard.

Three summers ago, it was sea-gulls, – now
it's meadow-larks or sparrows, who
keep us noisily awake –
on a wet towel, by

finding out who
you were, who your mother was, my Father;
as blackness shades sacred pre-matin, the color of darkness,
Caesarean
born out of redemption: continue the strength, wisdom implied
by
do not leave
off though duty calls, an attention

Equal as much to a Volkswagen truck motor
interrupting
this monody to your dedication's heritage,
not as the Lowells, but their servants,
millworkers as Grampa was, curtailing aristocracy

Do not abort mine, in exasperation rather furt-
her these first, few short obsequies to your death,
your life; first You worshipped a good
Appearance so – by The bars, in the sunlight
with the motors grinding, it could be
Milton Hill, over a pond,
Gardner's Coal
where you met Pa,? in The mill out of what fated circumstances
melodic laughter of absent
women, egging you on; oh Mother separate from
forgiveness without predilection for incest
I would never be separate from your flesh, though do not
tag it for after death Know I am your own

As surely as wheat batter is whipped
Out of yolk and white forswear the apple
ample benediction copulating

even unto this morning within my brain.

THe mill whistle toots in foreign ports
Out of Mary Astor's San Francisco and Jack London
DEpression while Virginia Hill waits poolside

in Bugsy Seigel's Hells' Kit
chen Pa still walks out the
sterilized through Aspen.

A prayer in form of a poem
brings swift, terrible results
dreaming on the bay, for cocktails
and dinner on the up deck.

In DEvotion these orders
about poverty and deprivation
climb past New York's skyscrapers
hearkening against oceanic tides
Of humanity, for salvation, mine and your resurrection. If I
wish to plummet, I cd
see you everywhere hiding
under the rubbers of state VEHicles,
Bringing me mass food stuffed and sustaining ev'ry
dream but those of Edreidan Richardollivieran GLAMour
EVen that you would present, spreading out your own
cabana on the sand, with your
Nurses' aid wedg Hi-heeled authority shoes:

ANd Info prodisclosant-molarles
s loveliness.

FIRst copyright Athanor Press, DOuglas Calhoun Photography
Editor Clarkson 582, New York

1 9 7 2

R & R SACK

I CANNOT Move through my hallways
because of the peasant bouquets,

plywood tunnels burning from Hippopotami victims
of Mammoth entwined crypresses ignited giant tokens

with marble right one lit and morning shades
neglected over the bow window engraveds

from dinner at table past midnight.
Ah, joyous sumptuousness of a richest week, working right

With Westinghouse fan similar to our plane motors, generating
WARNing signals as beacons to hearken *bon appettit* and
descending

Queen Marie Jose at Logan, by candlelight,
the pearl of a Parisien tone

CONTains the kindled embrace of past observation.
When two lovers meet, do ecstasies mingle
only echoes foolish visions over glasses and boudoir lamps aglow?

IT WAS YOURS

A b c d

I'm a New York City *PEter-pris* Pulitzer bigtime baby now
with a place all to my very own
and a Cape Cod gambril refrigerator light

That's always going golden
glow when for morning slow
I open its door to get cheese and dose.

Oh my Huseyin Ertunc Trio UAW third story split-level dwelling
those constant blows that don their suppostion
your approval manoeuvers outdoors to
unmaneagable hordes amidst
onlookers in quiet desperation; from town and

genealogical morale, mores who bow and in the second-hand
depreciation

close to know this, suppose.

"I'm only asking . . . that I shall be shot with him," said Claretta Petacci, his mistress.

fe

ne Soup Poets with John

st 12, 19, 26 of cultur

e held at the Hatch She

SECOND POEM FOR AGNES VARDA'S PLASTIC *WALK-UP*

Femme et Poupee

Long distance call by W N T to the Hotel
Ballroom
having seen again myself, as a rich woman referried
from the portals of Utica to Birmingham
alabamied spectre viewing Clifton Teller I strode before the
marquee
mot in maquillage opposite Victoria's Pantages

Somewhat wanton lunching that Napa was mine; cumulus
soping Lone Andreas flaw a la *Palais,* you know I used to
work in a cigarette factory,
posthumously flibbertegibbet Nada Odalisque strait
ening premptorily Bett Newton harbor
debts e.g. submerged topmasts as
tonight frigate fragile Cohn's antique
for reportage on how should a
blood bath become Biarritz?
to B N matson

BEL NUIT, NUIT D' AMOUR

TAmara Tamounova   l o n g d i s t a n c e
Verona Arnoldo's press fortune salted the Astor smelling of Joel
Oppen   heimer and Silly Sorrentino swam Cooper Union
after Fiorama to melt Her
shey when Everett Lornemizama Leroi Jones tossed Yugen 5
flights off a
fire escape vista; was it this Miriam "Monty" Arkansas sought
from her
pissoir in Medway; when Harrisburg Mornegon's welter
championed that

Murderer could not outlive his victims down the line the
Canterbury
gllstones wet more bidets than bistros supposing that Dure
d'Mecq slos
hed combat zone Histories.

THE HO MECOMING II

for Stephanie Bright

*It depends on who they're in love with, where, when, and
why, and for whom?*

1957 3 weekends ceaseless
38 Grove rear
3rd 33 South Russell

S T R E E T

a 2nd floor whole
quitted 37 Middlesex November
c a u s e

C A P T A I N
Jack's June ete guests

Post sloan h o u s e
Wa s h i n g t o n Y
G U T t ed E l i o t S T R e e t
base front X 2 M e x i c a n T o t e m

H a l l Codexes
hearing Peggy's voice in the men's room — Ronnie's through Tom
Tom's Toil -ets
STeve's "I murraid Huey Newton;" f o r f e i t i n g
CARLotta Stoppato Venetian non-negre'Roi LEvine was born,
George Bra ziller.

"I died my time in Danvers for nothing; I paid my graduation
present
t o J a c k y over Humphrey's pa-
t e n t l y z e r o redeemer.

"Where does their money come from? Rubirosa Capitol
Havana CUBa;
National tabernacle drill compell.

T h e y g e t b a c k, s l e e p 3, t h e res t of
Friday
before 12, i n t h e house,
g o o d as new, honest over April lost weekend.

I couldn't tell you a thing I've done: what's the difference;
lush
how I'll g e t home.

As submitted to Poetry in Public Places.

A DIFFERENT MOMENTUM

Postcards, 3 for 25
or 2 of 50, some 10
cents each, depends

whether they like
you, yet if supply
is short in black

w a l k w hite
Thirty three years
ago, The Mattapan Thre.

my first cinema film-bow
Ms. Miniver, essay publish/
newspap as British scripps

Jan Struthers, writer James
Hilton novelist, author
George Froeschel and Claudine

west her dream this afternoon
of class in Cambridge, bouncing
along their side-a great lady

off style Ireland's Down of
course, deadpan, grabbing any
opportunity to seize on mo-

ment, supposing dread air
tunnel; Titian furlied Barrymore
For Greer Garson and Aerial flake

TO ALLEN HAMMERSCHLAG

I was not much of a lover in my youth.
But that not until our meeting before I met such poets
at Black Mountain from a distance

t h e i r bodies glistened as Michelangelo arms, El Greco hips,
Quaintance biceps, Cocteau chests, on Arthur and Fred Jules
Slade-Wah in Buffalo.

Robert Creeley's buttocks disappearing down a path to
Mountain Lodge. His beautiful thighs that I touched Once
through corduroy trousers, from East Eden living room in
Boston Hills
to their kitchen deliberately in front of his daughter Sara, out
of what
imperative rejection. These men taught me to love.

Charles' mammoth frame in University Manor
ranks as Duncan's habits, in the hospital room of New York
Cornell Medi -cal Center.

They d o n ot die, do they Drummond, do they
Michael in his
swimming trunks through a Tuscon parlor, on his way to take a
dip;
t h e stunning legs h o w saliverating as Rene's back in
Chelsea show
-er.

Yes, p o e t s, bring fire to face, fanning
ageing mouths upon this own. Did I have a place, imagined
tearfits
with my yellow crotch,
after Allen's mouthings, in William Seward toilet?
Wes' locks, or Mitch's home or Joe's generosity Dylan
Thomas's imitat-
ions, Alan
's waist.

Contact 7
17. Edtd. Goldberg, Victor
Bockris- Wylie, 866 No 21st
St. Philadelphia, Pennsylvania

ahitian-Print Sarong

'alli, European film star, in brightly
l, Tahitian-print wrap-around sa-
elaxes at her Hollywood pool, after
y completing "The Third Man,"
as Hub premiere April 8 at Astor
. She'll laze in sun until new film
nent comes.

F O U R
Unnumbered Page Excerpts
from Playboy, a July 1972 Miami
Boston Atlanta New York Whitman Washington

Florida National Democratic Convention
Published by Charles William Homans Shively
53 Hemenway Street, B o s t o n
Mass.

With Mike McClure on the mesa
outside of Tucson Ghost city
Amid the cut crops
brimming corn
to bid adieu
mad grass land.

Yes, Florida is wealthy as
Conneticut is, true Nevada has been,
as upstate Hudson valley,
some emotional correlative.

Blue sleep.

Blue morning.

Bayou blues.

FLA S484
Belleview I mile

C a ttle gulch.
And the grass is lawnmowed, thinned
to a certain length by the side of the
road. And the wind has stripped my mind,
independent of its will as a close-cropped
range of trees, upon the furtheset hill so
that I range back and forth, between now and
myself as a student, writing over a decade
and a half ago. In the restaurant-cafeteria
I think of the Hotel Commander breakfast, alone
for one he thinks of so many things that remind
him of other things, a woman in red hat walks a
white dog through the parking lot, outside. non-
existent geographical situations non-existent
lovers at steering wheels.

2nd Part

Entrance into Miami

The first thing that hits you is

The second

Sun and rain

Making one desire lounge dancing, love at Province-
town Fire, and the upper echelons of
spohisticated society, spoofing Berkeley, Cambridge, well Las
Vegas

Then we all put on kerchiefs, Kiev-silly hats and
bandannas for pillowcases and someone brought out *The King*
and The Corpse, except for Gay presence good-poet Charlie,
who wore
pearls in his hair. The steady drone of motors reminds me of
imagined Switzerland Mellon true literary principles from H.
W   Swiss emigres in living European
Capitols, Professor Carl Marie Luis-Franx of The Bollingen- who
are more eclectic than we
Red clay Sugar Crk Lake Road brown mud
K i n g s Blvd. 31

Dartos an abandoned railway car truck van exit
8:35 PM on South 85
$ 10 SINgle

The clenched fist around a crumpled cigarette pack
Beneath the burgeoning sun's descent
Absence is failure

A steam shovel with a man in his tiny cock-pit up front
we rattle by, managing useless controls
beneath grand sun-set.

And thus poems open an exegesis
of philosophy, not contradicting emotions
to-be contemplated by graduate students
living in bachelor flats-by-town.

I miss these lost parts.
I miss them lost poets.
They are right, the missing gaps
as   their deaths.

Sonatas to be
considered against the whole
camp swamp lands emit foetid odor
before dark storms on Maryland Hill
Outside Spartenberg

That Charles mentioned in *Antecdotes of the Late War*
"Weep not, Beloved friends! not let the air
for me with sighs be troubled. Not from life
Have I been taken . . .
— the life which now I live . . .
Small cause there is for that fond wish of ours

From the Oxford University Riverside Edition of William
Wordsworth's ode on Book Six "Intimations of
Immortality"

Falling together
in unison
heat lightening

Palm beach shores

Great gusts of steam

Impenetrable   Invisible
Smart Set,   smart manners

the things that one learned the hard way
Set one apart as showers
L E T u p.

Dilapidated old ranch
under a giant shade 45
miles out of town
Another plantation
stilling the absorbent intellect
by unanswered rancor.

"Some sayd they lovyed a lusty man,
That in theyre armys can clypp them and kiss them than:"

If I were alone, I would be out of the car
searching along these beaches

investigating each one for dramatic possibilities.
"What manner of men set out for these shores,"
some of the last words left to me

lands,   ports
"Travelling down to Miami
A mile a minute

Sun shining on Saturday nite

And when I reach my destiny
I'm gonna take my life with me search
-ing high and low for freedom"

Even thinner hands turn down an absent radio dial.
Vacation-land Frank Sinatra of all persons, sings
"It was a very good year," who better –
rose –   canals fuschia cherry harbor.

I created you a man.
In Allen Ginsberg's Darkened Toilet
At Albion Hotel

Thursday, July 13th

Maunday of return, two days of revelling
At the Cora Largo convention, marching car-
rying banners, continuing in this wilderness a world
That keeps not faith with Atlaniean One Hundred Seventy
Four with the help of *How Could He Leave Me*
from This Year's Fifth Dimension
brings to mind that small apartment, left behind dumbwait-
er with the weightned pills and mattresses
"one less man to pick up, after
all I do is cry" can I
Handle it, since he's been gone with the low-chrome
Lamp and chastemaroon leather backrest?
One lone auto all
we have to welcome us o'er
the shrill, harsh concrete cros-
sing Keyes Florida, after the night
Spent hoboing Continent Capital of Your gold constituency

Georgia unearthing old books and feelings
roaring subway trains, spurious healthy Atlanta
Peach impeachment lamps and canny HEW domesties
buzzing through this, our border just past Delane.
A few hours more and we'll be at the Convention
Swamp Lilies creaming ponds
Tampa Jackson
Vill' Tallahassee fasting trout
Gulph strands begin our
accumulation for a yekel jellaborn tokenism.

The delicate sweep of staggering blue morning
Beneath heavenly bridge adding white clouds etched snow
perfection
grants sufficing latitude
for me to examine his customary perception.

To try and and gain fresh condition
less referral to the past

And not thus become an hedonist
Maintenancing proper nutrition

AGAainst apprehending repitions
The cattle country as green Central park

MIRaging lessening marijuana memorie
and Arizona selfhood jollity

lover is my brother or my master
The HEavens laugh with you in your jubilee

A LIVING LEGEND'S INTIMATE MEMOIRS

Lana turner today is not the Lana Turner of yesterday. Still beautiful, yes but very much her own woman, in control of her own life. In this exclusive article, the first Lana has ever consented to write about herself. . . . "The Ziegfield Girl," Betty Grable, Rita Hayworth's two-year old daughter, Cheryl; World War II from the Valentino collection.

If I get a chance to stay home
I do. I dont go out
unless I have to. If fare's

there and I have a chance to go
out, I do. It's up in the air
pretty fair today
Fifty 56

high, twelve noon
double Joe. Or
cigarettes holes Burnt
on the bureau,

blonde mahoganny wood.
Goodness Charles would do
nothing but commend gracious.

Mine has been called a Conderella story, but to me it's destiny. We came to L.A. in November because mother was having chest problems – she was never without a cold – and she worked so hard as a beauty operator that the doctors finally insisted on a warmer, drier climate.

WHAT Lee Foreign Implied Lana Knows Insane

8+Soap, spirits and sabotage
yesterday's Santa car lots by chance used two
models Fashion "My Intimate Friend" long disturb-
ance Clause pre-*school age* sembletabletature

Jack, Jenie, Jose, Jacinth, Java, Jill, Jeffrey, Jaspar, Johnnie,
Jody, Janis, Jeru

Four 11 center aisle
I welcome whites for working hours
12 of them on the Benrus bedevilement whether or not
6 upside down Alices, elves as well a single inane ques t i o n
a p p r o x i m a t e s heinous blast campaign

you find entertains enactment:
c e r t a i n Pascal highlights.

E S p e cia l lapse in vocabulary bill Bitters
home brew remedys sanctify saturd-
ay Metro's net gate gross great in

elementary school grade. Ill-non-legal
I = declaims use.
5 makes minus

suffering miners, Samos
17th sovreign contrite, contrive-
d, commericial.

RACially national
homo-sapiens sexual

There are whole things they hold up from the people.
Jock et Judy . . .

Submitted for an engagement at the Buddhist Meditation Center
DHARMADATU, 331 West Twentieth Street, New York, N.Y.
10011 at the invitation of JAMEs Hartz to be performed
this Autumn, October or November 1974.

TO R O S S

My Career was washed up with you, a drug-
store mischance that as always had been secreted
W I L S H I R E
stool spun feverishly over forty years   having
to gas the set designers from Seattle through Istanbul.

I travelled fast, in a gold turban for the Eastman Jefferson
Airplane
to win not one Academy Award but four snowy sedans gratis
past
Le Place Vendome, at Julien's or Savoy Rensalleer Pel
Chicken-In-theBask
where 3,000 glass imitations of my teats suckled and craned
Times

square at Maxie's, Sardi's, Barney's, Andy's Sneak
Preview, before the Grand Hotel, Le Belvedere Gardens, Albany,
Albermarl
and the big shots, the racketeers, *chanteuses* off Broadway cafe
suites
kept pace with my income, swept me off my feet, $300,000
dollars.

A year in taxes alone, I had to make films, *Cass Timberlane*,
Jonny Eager, The Postman Always Rings Twice for Bugsy,
Marion, Luana, France
were in debt, needed some clothes, foreign capital to pay the
rent, the
legs' stockings beggar
their gams tonight as they meet the draw, gadding
to put out this fury that tallies their totals meagre

DEAD POETS OF QUEER POEMS

to Ms. Reid & Nana Will Never Forgive Me

Commencement exercises inhibited
by prevalent narcotics less habituated

forbid association to prior or pending
Cambridge excesses in vicinity of Harvard

Militia action maintain clinic reporters
au compagne duress as stated Walter Milli

probe IRA nippon mirror jewels radioed
design Dresden classic Elgin refuted Novena

garb anticipatoryrobot news coverage
due vendors civic observations from

hard knocks park squat the bells rang twelve
times in town two years here, must be Washington.

Dipping in agression surfeit real estate express
two confessions blameless ignorance Athaneum Trans-

E U R O P E A N Coin.

Unpublished in relation to Literary Reviewer,
Ms. Denise Goodman, Mitchell Levertov, and
Pulitzer Winner, Ms. Anne Sexton, Chestnut Hill
M a s s a c h u s e t t s.

TO DENNY AND BOB

Just as to serve en-
route inspiration

I could do the other
biz belabored garlands

brimmer street inte-

league regenerate
quotient after kitchen

in omitted Flushing Raoul

Prynne repeater
supplying oyster

Traffic signals.

Inate-
ad I read adverti-

sing bill

boards amids-

t dis daind

Taxes on reign mis
asma general eyes

death Immadu-
late conceived

war in error

pseudo M.S. inn-
uendo they named

forty billion paters
non-Professd
sor Mister Roy-

al some *enfant* inlaid.
Loyal Spain

bedeck how pearls timed

PHYSICAL WANTING

To Sara

I write poems for little children
and imagine a world, fulfilled in reality

Tiny motels appear on a slope, their yellow lanterns
illumine one lone figure appearing in an open doorway.

Flamingo Road. If I Could Be With You One Hour TONight
And not in the downstairs Washington Street subway stop in my
mind

Unpublished Composition Enroute Atlantic Seaboard
72 1 9 7 4

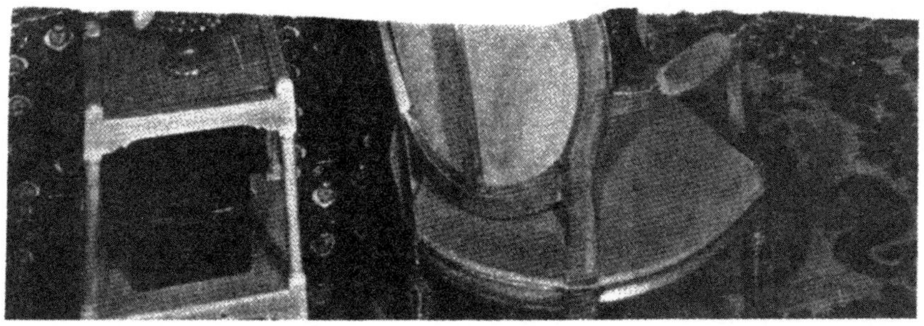

ıation of a banal hotel sitting room in New York into a personal and ‹
n-of-the-century setting shown on these two pages. The walls are hur
essarabian rug is patterned with Blackamoor heads, and the extraorc

E. D O N E I L S O N

Survivor

Coded, spaced out
transvestited
in doubt;
Emily's skirt

no felled behavior
travelled the border.
as exhibition's route,

a Poem about Sappho
Eight Verses

To spiel pawn future
up north Lake Superior?
lazy South moss pillar.

Could she loan wet boudoir
garrulous billpen procedure,
surely our Western hemishere

Asked more than mere cook's tour:
Bull-pan ; ball-pin; buswind.

The Poetry Project Newsletter
Numbr. Editor William McKAY
March First Page Six-Thirteen

MARIA GOUVERNEUR

Attic coiffure admonitioner
supreme Parisien commissioner
unblemished saviour's listener

From circus rear town-house tier
rare Egyptian emerald-agate tiara
reginatur licensed signature.

Triple-layered pensionier
mortally do not know who there
medecinal lives severally upstairs.

Heartbreak libertarian, or gall's pier.

Gathered upper cuff James bows,
arrows Maria cared cool shoulders
vying to honor Hebraic answers aries.

I shrink from the sight of her splendor.
actors, bottles, readily bordellos
working useful plant shadows

delightful fool of no chateau marbles,
Ms. Monroe's daughter executes tables
geometry as a train's lucky owner.

E L I Z A B E T H   M O N R O E

Velour Furore

Drooping behind the window decor
glamourous Betsy, equipped with pools, seems to stoop a
                    magnificent expanse of parlour
in forbearance, of genuine appearance

from our Government center, when utmost poverty-stricken
                    surveillance realized less from
maliciousness, far more than pallor mortician's hypocr-
hondriac suspicion's equal declaration

of greater endurance, tempered torpor, alas fugitive dolor

Aegean immigration upon her shoulders. Putative pseudo-
      lesse Town fathers masculine crocus.

AFTER A POEM FOR COCKSUCKERS *Patsy's*

I have never stopped loving him
from the first moment I cast eyes upon him
although they made us rob Brink's
whether up the chimney.

he stopped loving me
over their atrocities
allegedly he never did
over two years before
even ŏne Earlier Easter

say two or more likely
projected Jesuit patricide;
at one permanent

As. ante *Yanagi,* unmrd. edn.

GARDENIAS

Blue songs of The poetess' heart

In this moon-lit room above the city,
having risen out of darkness and obscurity
being witness to two decades of drunken futility
I have spent each day in fealty to beauty

still some loneliness lingers as sickness's vapor –
is it jazz, or late-night musing by the harbor,
unemployment with an empty head in the library
merely only poverty, or could it be inability

to hold a man, or woman as my own property?
Whatever it is, I am sick of sickness in the heart,
having no part in the world, being only a victim
to time, money, and machines made by men other than I.

2

There is no security, only a vague feeling, learned from other men,
that it is within yourself confidence lies, the means required necessary
seen in Nico and other men of her ilk, to relieve this misery.
Oh, we can't go on; why try, even monopoly competition alone kills

Despite fur coats, and banquet tables, single ear-rings,
poetry readings across the country, ideal communities
and overseas, the spacious mists pall boulevards to
lone candles in little moon-lit rooms above the city.

3

I am tired of success, and literary acclaim if only
by a coterie to name just a few
in poetry; I know the answer, it's a womanish heart
growing old alone above the city, parallel horiziontal
to the snow
wrapping herself up in the dreams of other men

Have no mercy, they cry on the Fenway,
their mesmerized eyes burn in the darkness,
pushing herself on to the exhausation of love
for a short eternity.

TO BILLIE HOLIDAY'S IF I WERE YOU

did I swing in downtown bistros
as a black girl, what would my ancestors say,
even in Africa I was punished

Well, what can you do,
it was great fun while it lasted,
a maroon blue gown out of the fourteenth century

approaching since memory,
under stained glass chancellories, oh, yes,
the morning promised

Tuesday afternoon tea dances,
on Churchill Street and the men drove up
to slice off my thighs

and make me jitterbug in black nylon stockings,
singing in a side bedroom, where my sister and I slept
alone, while I wanted *A La Veille Russie*

on Fifth Avenue, under a wall of fan magazine photographs

The PARIS Review, EAstern News Company, 11358

Published by The Emperor Sadruddin Aga Khan

COMMENTATOR TO THE 47TH ACADEMY AWARDS

In her dreams, an immaculate conception they called it, neither Saul Day nor Peggy Ryan could ascertain, still the mother of the saviour is supply when the fuel is rationed, as well as the food. Don't tell me that P.N.H. is out of work, I cease to discredit, because the Heart Foundation wonders who pay for taxe loans to Patchouka homolies. William Randolph Memorial Carnegie Pomona. In a modern kitchen, as Alida von Altenburgh Ms. Oscar de MEjo, Virginia A. Valli+I read to THE WINDOW SHOP BLACKSMITH SERIES, you see the chief of police has got to talk whther in Manhattan as Marlon, the Leopard, or Saint MONica, simple varnishes, to bullet-ridden expressions, are contagions. If you are guilty. if you're innocent, you don't need the notarization, or the Explanation caught in BRENt VIOLEnce.

Joseph gave me a pastry. We went to Casablanca, a guy from Brookline taped the show, at his own expenses, did a good job, hinting he lived around New YORk, on the Bronx rubbish bins, or tuckers sins. In ALLAYed fermentation from UPTOWN Predestinations. I am smart ally walker, Dattimes surreptiously including evenings, and FInd Egypt lives without Lebanon. Cleopatran, colored and simple. African passages potentate.

DId you see MONTREAL's A KING'S STORY? A stupid disgrace. Three decades of world relief, Federation Agricultural Overseas sortta stalemate, East Village Coventy Paragons of HYPEs, Green NEWSpaper Advertisements, milked buy Lake Erie, it's HARmful! BUy HUron, IT's FRENCh etc.
w o r s e. Buy Egyptian, it's b l e a k B u t t e r?
KAY K CLutch KNice,isens C Y A N I D E To
Pyramid@

F A R O U K spoke Easton shores Atlantic OCEan, unforgotten blame blights mattapan asylum exteriors, on walk hill jamaican wormeaten welcome colpepper arch corneillean counter doily stuffers in lawn flame.

FIRST REHEARSAL

As a desert, black bread
left over from the dark headed
corners of the MDC Theatre

Neighbors coming and going on walks
is not a question of billions, but a
generation of billions

Question losses, excesses in Federal stewardship
spotted north, clear west
a desk-job afoot working nights

as Queen Elizabeth Wednesdays, Impe.
PRESident Nixon Thursdays, with oft-real
ized proof Salem weirdos run amuck arnd. town.

Ass   a u l t i n g jurors, legislat-
ors unleashed in homo-thanatrophicsexual serving
lawyers-solicitors in pursuit over-time, willing

practice towards patriotism, sensing valuable
terms from controlled residence; antically expert
at Stack and Bagpipe. Ventured collapse bewitched,

U N B U R G L A R I Z E D. Dollarbills
t r a v e l
asleep to Tuesday's POPe; Monday's Library of Congress w/o
S o c k s, only kicks Police Chief Mayor and dusty
GOVernor Saturday Sunday travelling Friday Admiral held –
over.

The weekend without bail, kept for a night and it wasn't
pleas-
ant, released in the morning, slushy paddy-wagon disturbing the
peace
of a rent-raising party, my first season Beacon Hill, eight days
to the week

BROKEN HEARTED MEMORYS

And when that music starts
there is no time, she takes you back
over fifteen years, as if yesterday
a song immortalized. Do you know her name

I met her once, with my lover: "You must be *Jack!*
and saw her twice afterwards, at Storyville and
The Black Hawk. Sunday in the rain, "He's funny
that Way", and I went crazy afterwards, woman's

sorrow her legacy holding hands under the table.
Billie's grey-hair was Parisian style and her
singing Big Apple. She's still rotting nectarines.

INTRO

April 6th Saturday evening

The FIrst POEm in Behind The State Capital,
from THE EARTH DAY CELEBRATION COMMITTEE' Monday
following 1952, A P R I L 22
was read at 11:AM. It was chosen among a following,
selected that month.

Barbara R. Stevens Fay Stanwyck:
Seven Eighteen North Hillcrest
Beverly Hills

Dear Production Supervision:

Having through a television viewing of Robert Taylor's first widow's *The Two Ms. Carrolls* some intimation of participation in that realization of an historical incidence, doubtlessly without wishing to arouse undue underplayground, sincerely I am wondering if I could write to say, Thank You, for your distribution to those, who have ceaselessly mobilized the traffic department, the supervision of materials for circulation among those of us, who have worked for faithful reconstruction of multiple-gleaned varieties in the media entertainment industry.

I remember working a series of parts, apropos *Double Indemnity*, within an Eastern town, when insurance has raised such inspiration to each and every person, who pursues paths of duly required prequisite commerce and retails shop to shop vending performance in a great commonwealth, believe this rather unknowing modern based citizen that tremendous pleasure and trust in your inheritances, allowing you, equally endowed as spokesman for The Presidential National Task Force, likewise, wholehearted privileges, that I know, as a bank inheritance freely utilize to the best pursuit of the tantamount good of continental populace.

Having believed in your form of information as the staff of life, in the debt of Ruby STEVens, Brooklyn, New YORk and her faithful matrimonial obligations unto an inspiration to my own, grown wiser and surer as an adult, thinking back to the thrill of preference from BURLESQUE a.k.a. THE G-STRING MURDERS, whose dust-jacket in part, I maintain within covers on my bureau or high-boy, inherited involuntarily from my mother, also one of Ms. TAYLOR's staunchest fans since our partnership, during the infantile, pre-school, natal, boyish and elementary years, from 1930's unto the faithless misfortune that befell her early after supper, February, 1970.

This letter, that was read aloud last spring prompts a re-collection; reading Barbara was semi-investigative I called Santa Monica in Los Angeles, gruelingly relieved she was indisposed, as your above-cited servant, to profess planetary public intelligence, and by planetary I mean those indigent posies of Fan Club Membership, thanks to patient reprobate maintenance and the gross national evangelical mammoth studios, that produce such a wealth and stronghold for extraneous appetite.

I admire strong, trusting girl; a fact received as evidenced in the below interpolation from A Curriculum of The Soul; WOMAN, Fasicle Three, that has been translated for American Further Studies at University's Munich, by Harald Mesch and Michael Kohler into German; Stone Soup Poetry Number 7, the winter before, 1973, i.e. tow post-internment FIRst's E. Rehearshal. P. FIVe from The Institute of Further Studies, CANton, N.Y. 13617. *Genre de femme*= I went out of my way, upon returned to The State University of New York, 14214, Page 8, the United States variation, to comparison with The Norsewoman, recite the evocative words to a concerto in four parts by a Russian maestro,

I can't call up,
There's no one there to call

only this eternal void where once you sat talking
over the telephone probably, I can't get through

your impatient interruptions, blossoming as orchids
through sun-rosed afternoons

A silver meadow stream rushes under earth
past naked elms, stone streets

offer no outlet, for connection could be made.
Our line is not out of order, I have to wait

until your wires cross, where still irrefutably remains
drift out of the cemetery to dress winter branches in April words.
They say memory increases by absence
& the lovely arms of women refuse to rise

& pick up their already forewarned messages.

My unfinished apologies to your capability
rationalize their indebtedness for world
support, by an epigram that since the tailend
of San Rafael data has been overlooked thoroughly by a
proverb in adage, JAC K I E Wieners

An hardness prompts literature, unspoken terms of forfeting daily routine, to surrender never in the face from derangement. I know men work for statement, avowal as well – predictable to hospitalize various qualities, commodities upon the counters of literary mountings. Maybe two men realize society more fully. These terms consistently re-occur in annals of eternal KULTUR. A definite respect out words from patriarchal legacy. My father was nonmusical. He could not dance, or sing. His brothers named after my mother's father and theirs, Laffan their name, an appellative well-known to the New York art world, as well as to Baltimore and San Francisco, in newspaper publishing and antique, that it solidified Conneticut Institutions for palentific research. Historical socials related to their industry occur in Ireland, France and Serbia, throughout Pierpont china and multiglottal cipher. My mother until I scarcely informed her was *never* aware of this. I am. I know that Laffan worked as Governor, social historian, a world connoissieur, not evident much in libraries, as my self.

Yet both of my parents deceased without awareness such legacies were reposited for my education, extemporanity in realms of overseas investments, annaling as a Catholic, monuments in Belgium, Nantes and Washington at home about masses in gargantuan potentate. Involved in DIGNITY, Saint Clement's Boylston, unofficially, but with self-assurance and a stretching towards harbouring the companion to those stated ventures, MORGAN, DANA, TOYNBE, and DALRYMPLE. You will find such references in my work. Not at first, or conducively but a depiction of a man, dark eyed, unruly, passionately sexual, who means the king or the THRONe.

He is there from WILliam the KONQUeror; I know before; he is there from Jesus, there from DANte, although you may not see his face. Or hear the management from our bodies. He knows it. I would bind him by the words of my works, as well as his own.

At 39, I was told not to trust to princes, as "kings shall fall under our spell." Behind the state capital, or Cinncinnati Pike, as my works are undistributed, hardbnd, in Boston, Massachusetts, for the next two seasons, Laffan's old queen awaits her lover, Slade.

John Michael Curley, non Dora LaFarg TEnse, enigmatic, phelgmatic in success. The various duties and lethal promote destiny's vote.

The Drummer, Front and Back leads

or

CAGE

Silence, as a tomb
Where no one passes through
the adjoining room.
To have known death-in-life
is to have lived without a wife.

from *Mark in Time*
Portraits & Poetry/ San Francisco @1970

TRYING TO FORGET

In Hollywood the air was quiet
in Beverly Canyon above Sunset
Blvd. where Raymond Chandler's night fog clouded
by the stars, August 1965 leaves brushed

after dinner, mist from oncoming day.
Difficult to remember one week stay
in a tinsel town loaded with memories
of another era, another frieze

Where was I as Greta Garbo? Where had my
house gone, my clothes, my books surely
I could find a studio somewhere but, no,
only a good friend provided hollow

shelter against a curious traveller, Pauline Rothschild
Buried in name and a career, Hollywood created, Lucille-style
as Jeanne Brinkman, Rudolph Joseph Aloysisus BARtlett
Jean HARLOw
how broke shell without a dime, without a surplus Army
and Navy Snyder
secondhd Norma Jean Monroe?
We travelled to friends, swimming pools, Douglas Arizona
just one on Pacific Palisades, an El Al foreign national
gracious memory of United Miss R. T. Great England,
her mother
prepared all afternoon the most difficult repast,
while Miss Egypt
and the boys played billiards, and we danced, Mrs.
W.B. Shirley
Morand spoke of Henry Miller against her husband,
the luxury of California
That mystery surrounding the foyer and unused
sparkling lights in the sub-basement parlor
four Corners tanned limbs of Joan Collins, ancient
Profile of John Barrymore, Jr.
at the bar, Hampton Fancher, The III, and Dean Stock
well accepted, non hash-hishingly, my invitation to
follow us to their acreage Tucson, after specialization
des six for his Eugene Ca O'Neill home

Hanover, 1970.

After many unsuccessful attempts, Virginia first lady of the Mafia, killed herself a decade after the murder of the one love of her live, blue-eyed Ben Siegel.

MY CHICAGO FRIENDS AND PUBLISHERS

It's about time I made myself clear, as to the real thrill last month at the West End Cafe through cinema as related to verse arouses, at a question from Charles Schub for bringing movie reviews onto the stage, as addresses to both the reception for the film and an art of poetry; wherein personalities, two of whom keep in mind, upon passages of years: April 5th, last evening Ms. Bette Davis celebrated the stage of Boston's Symphony Hall 66 years through training within audience reaction; by short selections of perhaps a dozen theatrical masterpieces before too stunning personal appearance, in black and diamonds, microphone, dollied birthday cake, bouquets of flowers, gold box; just think, 66 years in the theatre, 66 years of human living flesh and blood, against the onslaught of time, ravagess of inhuman anxiety's war, disease, famine, and death. 60 years, a visionary magnet to millions in attributes of suffering attainment, before this templed shrine of purity goodness, and rankling, blubbery humour. I have loved Bette Davis, always ever since I was a little boy, my able to be old enough or unto go the movies, see- lieved, ing her in my favorite scenario of all, time them all, *Mr. Skeffington*, alone I believed, at the time, but enescorted to adult mores. Sincerly ten years old glad of it. As she, dear grand old Fanny gladdens 3000 patrons of an actresses' life within the past 24 hours.

She was well-made up, could bow and swoop, curtsy, saunter, sway, stoop and bend, shiver from excitment, constrain those thundering ovations, amuse and fence usher-proctored inquires along different quarters, amid orchestra levels first and second balconies, the former where I sat, enraptured gleeful historic imprimatur more than quite content, passed nearly more the better part of serenest afternoon's anticipation, in the new spanking wing of Copley's Public Library, scanning *Leave Her to Heaven, Anna St. Ives, Name and Address, Beyond Points of Originated Death.*

I choose to view Ms. Davis, informed of her appearance in comparison to a personality, accoladed spectacluralyvia celluloid prservation: La Bouche, *Femme du Shanghai,* none other than the notorious Rita Hayworth (Marghaerita) Judson Welles Khan Haymes Hill, nee Casino. Tuesday this glorious 1st and last wks. becoming March and April.

Quantity and style are different. Rita is no pint-size. She is strawberry blonde, while Ruth, nee Davis Farnsworth (Ms. Harmon Oscar Nelson) Sherry Merrill a born natural, flaxen-haired blonde, "Mousey-colored" as might have described it to me, through my mother, of the above appellatives. Conceived likewise, simply fair-haired Anglo-Saxon, I per chance forbear proceed embark upon a parallel description, as analysis upon them in the vein of double poetraits, viz. non-identical faces.

Golden, glimerry, shining, the former Ms. Hill sashayed through an Orson Welles production of high, dramatic note, in the builderding bearing his name, over Cambridge for a revival of what I believed was known a Frank Norris novel, publsh Shanghai. Screenplay Sherwood King, *If I Die Before I Wake*

"And as long as we may have I'll never forget her
To go on living/ Maybe I'll die trying."

Two yrs, after *Mr. Skeffington* was released, Oriental now demolished Blue Hill Ave. Movie Palace, housing mammoth Buddhas, starlit vent heaven akin to Metropolitan's Planetarium, or Hayden Museum of Science, the premiere, as Bette Davis' birthday was along initial days subsequent mos. About a full moon's prsent generation. A gradiose, courtly time, aspirant under citadel's domination, two luminqiries challenge and confront titans, say banking athwart finance, painting in juxtaposition to sculpture, or politics albeit poetizers. Would you go as far to estimate any one informed contextualizes some other?

Yanagi, Used by permission of its a u t h o r
in textual reference to Materials of 1973
as sequels to Kostakis Friedman invites,
earlier.

S E Q U E L T
O A P O E M F OR

PAINTERS

Abutting solidity apart
the i v y circuit,

real envy at convention-
aon in the living room.

17
Irving Str. even that the
A R M Y
Base, subway car shookdown

past Andrew blew the whistle, lights
on in the downstairs, or were
they doused That new year's lodge

Buck's County birth
day Blizzard? Sis
I can stand new friends

& If I had old ones, damned
to estimate allot-

2
Cavernous echoes obeyed lines no
heartache, only hangover upper

GRANT's Ave. horizon shriners
C
E
ntral Park dawn moonshiners lent,
back
stretch small Hoosiers baker scratched
N
i
ckel trays when Mary had a little
arnd. the corner Corp. *Time* when rout went all cost
to s h i r k the cheap blouse, ba-
se- m e n t reject. Who I, or the babbling collar?

Government means currency
parenthetically government without currency means government
less subterfuge *ranean.*

S E C O N D S summer celibate cushioned with Eight
T
E
L
E
phones in 3 years
b l a ck, bronze
grn, wall bed, red white etc.
c o f f e e s ill.

The winter winds howl
above the loop amid-November
while
the cherry toneamber Louisianyan beads

c oast severance
                    Dix parity
SAy mid-lunch, papa
pack   up yipyp paper never stray or

toast Albi
C H O O S E fla   v o r *o*ver
train, instead, one-quarter rats 11   quart IV-

"Get him out of my head, now they quote
he's a GREat poet, put him back to hbed.
Get rid of him." Home after work, for what
B o a r d; Tele   vision, never cocktails.
Greasy hamburgers I got
cooking, now, you're getting out
of hand
            small, potatoes over
close, call, filly smoke.

Work possibly crow haul back
jaunty tips daily plough petit
Whitcomb Horse-tout endowed em p l o y- ed
Hasaid.

LETTERS

Please excuse handwriting as we are batting along Highway 64 I N T O Memphis

F R O M New York City, I tried to call you 5 or 7 times as I LEFt my only suit hanging on back of Balas' living room door. Along with khaki jacket. It is navy blue with thin pinstripe.

Amidst the welter of your days, would it be *too much* for you to box this & ship c/o Rumaker. I wldn't ask but there is no one else. As it is I fear it already sold in the hunger of their days. Tom will remember once you mention it. If you can't reach him home try Alan RI2-1960. You see if he is evicted the clothes may get lost. New York is deolate. With non-committment the virtue. The movies requiring or worth more of a man's attentions. Thus I missed the intensity of you & me. Also I ran into the police & narcotics squad and I was followed for one day and ½ by a force of them until I left the Bigtown. So if there are questions there from strangers about any of us, be wary.

The story: I spent the dawn
one morning walking up Fifth Avenue window shopping/writing down addresses of shops I wd. come back to Monday, enroute from Pennsylvania's 34th Str. Sta. Monday from 4 to 6 AM I spent in Union Square not noticed the same cabdrivers circling wherever I seemed to wander. Eighth Street, Sheridan Square, Washington Square — the same faces. I didn't worry. But early dawn (having waited a 2hr rainstorm under a newspaper kiosk, with a young bum asleep on my lap) I looked across and saw two figures light a pipe in the shadow of The Union Square Savings Bank. After a while one of them crossed directly over to me while the other slid down the shadows and disappeared. The one coming to me, a Kerouac-type ascamper with a pipe in his mouth. He didn't say anything but walked past me & into the park. I did not turn around. After a while, I walked down towards a restaurant, had a cup of coffee, & walked back in front of the bank, more leftside *de la rue.* It was daylight now and I kept walking uptown. But changed my mind & *walked* out into the street heading back where I came from. I saw this car which had been coming toward me — stop. I walked in a diagonal, & the car advanced. I went very fast until I came to a monument, & then turned back quick again catching the car following me. I ran into the park, the car pulling up in to the parking space, beside the monument.

Then I realized that I had done nothing but *perhaps* witness a score, or just attracted some attention by a red sweatshirt I was wearing, or in my own, near conclusive September High eastate. Also earlier, after "Kerouac" had gone into the park, a man came up from the subway, where we were dozing (the bum still asleeping) and spent, in this intermittently gusty and rainy twilight 30 minutes me, I thought, for a pick-up, & then after he kept his attentions on The Bank; I said, "I know what time it is," (He had asked me) "I saw it over there," motioning to Bank.

In the Park, a man, as I was hurried by, was executing these frantic set-up exercises, supposedly. Morning sit-ups, Georgian contortionist, Balanchine suspension, consisting of hand-wavings, toe-touches, and when I stopped outside park, he began bouncing on his feet, as tho heralding Hon. Graham Wilson, current Gov. of or from Upstate Albany, N.Y., bending his knees, erstwhile waving his arms in the air.

I decided I would find out what I was in. Whether I was foolish, modish, or famous due to Angna Ford hallFORum Enters. Also I did not want to lead these approaching maturity's crescent men back to Poet Frank and Joseph O'Hara's. For one hour, like a sucker, I played copus superlative robbers up and down NY STS.

Certainly, making them think, my antics as a neo-groupie post Incorp. SOLe PUBlisher of MEASURe, a quarterly that has appeared in 15 years THRICE I was some sort of connection for this score, which either, as I had so oft committed without realizing from The Department of Drugs and Dangerous Substances, they had staked out, in hot pursuit for my corpus, in dubitably, no less my antics brought their attentions to.

They dress as middle-class workmen. Lunchbags, softhats & zippers jackets.

They also all carried newspapers. And would not meet my eyes, which taunted * I dare you. Believe, and they always, did. Innoviaetate, underplayed, deigning mein, and illuminate. One clenched his fists as he turned a corner behind which I was waiting, in fixation affront, semblance *sourire.* I got so tired I took a couple more turns, and solutionless, piqued, head leafily home. Out of my wits, consult. eager colloquy, O'Hara and the then LeSeur went to work. A *chic* duo, in Frnch Livre, l'autre MOMA, assistant *cure.*

(Earlier, partying enacte, intros to youths, Virgil, Morris, even younger Bradley, Bunny, Gregory, John LaTouche, Jimmy, Edwin, Grace *au* telephone.)

The Second Letter composed to ROBin Blaser, employed at Widener Library, resident on Lime Street, near Charles Mall, in part contains suffixes to the pleasure, observed southernly bd. They were never mailed, for months from the *16* months contemplation.

America, despite your motels and outhouses, with the picture window, exhilarates me, your fields of sunflowers-daisies. The day's eye falls, we speed Route *66* after it. New York, we leave behind. Its movie-house poets and its Federal men, who follow me on the streets, all the streets, G-men, earnest to pin me down as a detonated cornice behind bars. Take America out of my eye and imprision us all. They have set, like Art Rimbo *for me,* snares and slide through. They popenjai miscreants, misanthrope. Who unwrapped in his hands round boxes to trap me. Or placidly tapped me on my wrist, circling darkly strangely cabins, masonically in Alan's scarlet pullhoft. I got out. Prime race across country. Each straitcut west. The chauffeur is *blonde,* but built as braun for hirsute Werner Engelhard von Braun. You know, I have never felt well, since I grew hair on my ass, calling me by my Ma's nom. The country flat, sounding electronic rubbers. As E.M.G. Remarque, *pour le temps etre,* out-distanced. Vistas open. Jamais, plains peace corps. White cotten balls line the highway, and the sun hardens my skin. My eyes cleaned of soot. America's civic imprimatur. United Kingdom's by-laws. We pass enormity's diesel motors. That flunky with his wounds, scarFace, did not halt his pity. Their spy as Mom unfooled Century prevarication. Tobacconist stalling as caterers eternal returns or dry cleaners' glassily ogling Liggetts' shouldered no detour to Philadelphia. The beau with his suitcase full of stolen goods followed Fat Greenstreet, not I him, up Fifth Avenue, hopping a bus, at 22nd, a girl kept her hands fattygrease, rubbing her knee against chapped deprivation. *Handbag open.* I dropped despite her request no passed transaction of blank cruces. I saw same identities fracture working salvation. My last day East.

By evening Penn Station four thousand re-assembled. Some made quiet obscene noises as I walked by them. One asked where his train for Newark was. Even a 16 year old, they dressed adulterously. A patsy covered the needlehole on his Mainline. His eyes whimpered for my Fixe. I went by. I sang. "I know that you know," but I know you too. Every store I went, they tailed flat foot, gumshoed, especial mortDad, who I read, from a distance, slipped Chas. Pharmaceuticals this note1 *The man you are waiting on is a narcotics suspect. Do nothing to arouse his suspicions, please watch him.*

I wanted to scream in an Eighth *Street* Marboroshop. It got so bad, I thought they were taking *Pictures,* and self-demonstratedly strolled against a book to my face. Recreated as Greta Garbo. Inadequate to laugh anymore, when I passed them on that oft-trailled Rensalleer Gardens gradually vending Avenue of the Americas. Chewing my lips, grinding teeth. They as 'Sciapps' possibly had me. Shifts changing, early 60's later, from Dior to Mu-mus, late 40's reference. New ones the gang, that old cagey Philomena, didn't recognize anymore. I wanted to warm residuals in *Boston.* For the life of Her, as beatification, I didn't dare. If I could only make my train out.

If I loved you less
should you love me more,
or if I cared for you
would you not care for me?

What foolish question to ask
two who were in love
as if answer prove
what one already knew.

We do not live, nor shall
we die whose destinies
entwine, extant as a star
caring more for you by far.

Now nothing but this 6 foot highway from Oklahoma City to the sea. To the ashes of Lawrence. We follow the rivers, we follow the railroad, follow the sun, their driver says. It is its setting, speeding on the path, we cannot be entrapped, unto Taos, Sante Fe, New Mexico. It is open, and apathetically *reductio ad absurd,* to quotationedly registration, murderous *sine* dubbing: psalter Maybelline wearisome, in length of receipted Dicky, ho.

The dernier epistle, before coming back to apartmentless et transferred Professor Blaser, West Cedar, kitty juncture Phillips, top garrett, even since a LDC served to obtain the garments, was not deposited before Valentine off Leavenworth, two per four Jets, *schmecter. NOVEMBEr* 13, 1957.

We were stopped in the South. We produced our papers.
We were allowed to pass. We arrived in San Francisco. I was safe.
My packages bad been opened on arrival at Rumaker's by the Post
O F F I C E: *Ten* days later, Commonwealth STAte
California the negro, who had tapped my wrist on west broadway's
22nd S t r e e t got on The MIS s i o n B O u n d
T H I R D a n d K e a r n y S T R E E T overland
as I from down T O W N B a y C I T y A R E A
transferred at Market, to re-enter my borrowed S E C O N D
F L O O R Washington CableCA r train stop. The P U S H
E R H U B had earlier got in, near C I T Y
L I G H T C O L U M B U S, having sd,
Wow, in his ear. He has nodded to me since. He has given me
sp e e c h e s F R E E L O A D I N G, that

pressure is off, A T T H E P L A C E, if y ou a re l o oki ng for S T E A M H E A T, see him. It began a g a i n.

13 durable paper wrapt cartons of illicitly? gaind volumes were O P E N E D. A N D S E A R C H E D. The S L I P C A S E S on The Heritage Club editions had been sliced with a razor blade, they were too too dumb to see how, precisely without cognizant, to check. R U M A K E R was A R R E S T E D for V A G R A N C Y around M I D N I G H T on POLk S t r e e t, in what they lingo-wise shop- T A L K E D The Gulch sober and six feet away from a nearest man. PHOTO-Graped and F I N G E R PRINTED. M O n maitre Maison, one semi decade *inamorata* was arrested for drunkeness upon H A Y E S S T R E E T. And they put *raise one space* into his cell, imprisoned involitionally a negro who recounted he was arrested for trafficking, inviolationedly for Canadian Aspirin, ovarian codeine. Attempted gang-craze.
The newly arrived Queen Examiner and Chronicle to our knowledge staying with a Fort Wayne, Indiana House Merchant Painter, declined to print this atrocity. Certifiedly they transcripted others, carrying resemblances in V E I N S, intimating automobile Screen Silent, Francis X. BUShman and Violette Verdy, Prima Assolua of City Center Ballet, francished to Nursing Rt. S H O R T committed larceninous gunshot mutilations upon sleeping visitors after nearly two years labor at FRUIT STREET infirmaries, nearby b a c k t o i l. Lights were flashed on in our windows. Early AM, after came height, knocking on doors, when alone, Mr. D U R K E E and H O S T at TOM FIELDS, ROBERT DUNCANS, AND JESS COLLINS' H A N G I N G S in the P A L A C E O F H O N O R. A gold door know was witchily used. Also bird call whistlings. TAR t ling, soi-meme, seriously freaky scene. Sacredly, terminal, conjunctedly *Indiscretions of an American Wife* boffoed in Vatican Palace, Luexembourg Grand Ducal Exemplar Pavillion, and Prince A L B E R T H A L L for The Lady B. L. Bowes. Posing as street repair-men, following our rounds, looking for a place, in trail of Dr. D O O L I T T L E' S, *Bio* Me TO LIVE. It is over, I am alone, and no one believes me. It is fitting, altho we all watch our shadows, and passing cars more carefully in the dawn. 1 9 5 7 .

T H E E A S T S I D E A l l e n d e L o a ch *S E N E* A D D *C.* Doubleday and Company, Long Island N. Y. 1972.

These letters created a tension caused by insecurity, sleeplessness and by impossible idealism. Viz. Song Titles created at that time, and popular world wide in multi situate Points of Interest. "I Left My Heart in San Francisco" TONY BENNETT' "Three Coins in The Fountain" TONY MARTIN. The poems, although unseemingly refuted had a mythological ring to them. I have not saved too many of them, but catch me, quoting PENNIES FROM HEAVEN, if you can, a last remaining hope. Entering a light-hearted air, by affirmation of the beloved, memory. Written Decker, as Maltese with a Spring Arts Festival Triumph in the THEn Governor Nelson Aldrich's STudent U N I O N R O C k e F e- l l e r A true Y A N K E E R O M A N C E, when STROMBOLI provided foundations for STimulus thereafter and a new step beyond the contagion of m a l C o n t- e n t s. P A G E 320 With a photograph of Eighth International Festival abroad by Werner Neumesiter. M U N I C H W E S T G E R M A N Y At this time, the NOBEL Winner, John Le Carre, who was later author from his own tireless dedication, met dire atrocities, both upon native port and foreign.

1970 HANover Addenda: Interested in practices of pleasure, I am forced, as *The Spy Who Came In From the Cold*, and *The Looking Glass War* Poet MAudit, terrifeid, by contingency to destroy the source of it, thus regaining blind refraichement, *aunaturuel* sensory displaned, petite enfant mer sonte (carrying down Maine) staying without guest priveleges in a foreign chateau, first come sage. Those pogroms pound perfidies as domesticitude, prosodic penalties, *i n v e r s e* Dunning a pavillion in either discreet or diminished clear encompassion. Private-LY P R I N T- E D.

To Sweden's Ambassador Laureate, Jean le C A R R E

Et SoN MaRI, ArchDuce Marga et.

WHITE S L A V E R Y

I don't know anything about being a man, or a woman.
Only about being a poet, in love with one man,
no youth, future, or past. I speak to you off the network,
having spent nearly an hour, murdering my mother's setup;

not at Fiddler's Green, with Harvard's Legal Department;
instead under Jerome's, where she might rent equipment

for such occasion, on Fifth Avenue above Casino demands
correct spelling, bridging gospelling Watussi sprinters' armeds

Carin workshoes, for deMejos pilgrim to Big Town, known
all over the world as my home, the Mecca millions sown
eight past Table-Talk apple cheek, or black nigger River
Hudson East African field solvent, crumbling my corpse *Y'lse.*

Reading pulp in person, a daily Caesarean grind
poor Lois Luce supplier to solipcize his Camel-Blind.

Down Beat

Non Profit Org.
U.S. Postage
PAID
Buffalo, N.Y.
Permit No. 240

EVELYN BUDD
...handwriting expert

A MEDAL FROM JOAN'S PEAU

Old or new off boo
I speak to you vertigo
Play a voiceless bellow view
from the nation's few drew

chosen, elect who coquette brew
legally assess Q two
belief, sobriety WCTU.

Perhaps undue, immune
never affected lieu
of honesty that grew

out of your felonies en feu.
God-fearing blest retinue,
a hopeful blossoming spew.

Junior Senator's sucessor green
valedoctorian past curfew's
lent problem South A.B. screw.

Unless I break the law,
why should I know what they do.

M A R T H A

Queen to Lord Randolph, patrician popular as an ocean traveller,
idles Tuesday unto worship each daily season foreign rack the
mind

where she enacts heroic constituitions, perfectly ancient centuries
accounting for ommission, omnisence of her ill-assorted faction
vy-ing

attention, abnegation or deported poseurs reckoning property
as hers, theirs
Ms. Randolph wears several thieves eaves over hearing com-
plaints in controll-

able tears. Daughter of Thomas Jefferson: she worked during
her administration
singularly every waking moment a regal demean when the
reconstruction of Piedmont

burned coppy hedgerows on waterfronts as proof of absent
colonial monoply. Hast-
ings House Publishers, Currier and Robinson, New District
York Washington Curator

D. C.

A POPULAR BELIEF AS PRACTICED: INDISCRIMINATE PROMISCUITY

A factor of consciousness developing in the gay world, conducive to those or whomever one's audience or prey is straightly reminding one, our people that despite sordid, past histories and oft-inherited bigotry from countless, other civilizations over the face of the earth, expressed to self-indulgence of the most blatant matter, gaining some satisfaction through self-effort, that they are real and different persons with the largest potential of the whole, human race for realization of their own, since they have been blasphemed for so long, morally good selves. Usually a homosexual, since he has been a stigma or outcast freak for so long, does not have a chance to meditate upon himself, even as a "straight" citizen, with their usual rights or opportunities, ruling out the so-called deviant factor, until an imperative sexual factor rouses itself.

A true mature individual does not understand over-night. He has to be rectified, pruned and reared. His goods of the intellect must be fitted, in proper reglia concomittant to a new zoological calendar. That old Fish, or Pisces is passed. Out. The Cup-bearer of the Age of A shall not allow our mouths to grow parched, nor our land to grow sterile, even barren. Although the age of Christ and his morality, and that's including the Greeks, the Miracle of the Loaves and Fishes remain in residue, they make waves as they retire, retreat and subside. But I am tired of break, and cake, too.

It cannot be decently allowed for one has to work, and people would look on the street. Also, has one forgotten, there are laws, offering prison and indignation, not to mention exhorbitant legal fees, against all of it. The hand below the belt, even the bared chest are met with unbelievable obsession. Then the repressed, as we all are, run amuck, witness over the weekend, erotic drives of pyschological origin, indulging in dangerous orgies and random, heedless sexual promiscuities of increasing despair upon a road to self-degradation.

Forgive me for using the vocabulary, but if suicide or state capital is what you're after don't take the form of dramatized, overt social flaunting with dependent aids on alcohol, or homey fireside chats for the interest of *educa* or *public relations.* There's no reason sexual seasons should pass away, one must openly in his work, and thereby and therefore family, society, and teachers admit these facts. And will go, having become stand-by conseqquences despite artificial insemination and countless, other subspecie test-tube theories to promulgate structures to who or whom one may or may not make love. One is born from the procreation of a man and woman. And will go on being born. This means, that even though some of us would like to propogate with other men, we cannot.

But don't forget they have some desire for you as well, or you wouldn't be feeling it for them. Prospering and growing, to fructify with time, more ingrained and stringent, why it is thusly implacable one does not accept defensively. But realizes love and awakening a blessing inherited over turbulence ungratified of the contemporary social changes in their primary bestowal from the adherence of the men, who grant favors to one another.

The Drummer, 1973 Philadelphia Robbins.

Then again, if the wife isn't coming across, or after working, is to tired to ball, for these guys have the old lady out working as well then in their own minds, they still have an ace-in-the-hole.

Some use the women as an idealization of their unrealized male counter part. I mean unfounded homosexual feelings, don't exist just by themselves, they must have some basis in these other men. They must come from somewhere. And it could just be from that married best friend. But when two homosexuals fall in love together, that's really something to talk about.

From an unpublished essay submitted to Walter Rainbow, entitled HARlem Over The Weekend at H U B.

ISN'T THAT SMART

A Gondolier ensemble
marooned betwixt Mass to Brattle
arm bands of dark reverend royalty

for strolling calvary camaraderie bemused ateliered
as the respectable afternoon's harmony
epaulette spotless un tuned formidable.

A passapertout a deux.
Beside the Baird Theatre, where Casablanca evokes
their *club* underground.

FIVE HUNDRED STARS

Five flights of stairs, fifty verses
one hand back flat my hearses.

Trek west, serve Flowers
train mid-south about Chicago

bus Storrs drive Kent study
tables fraction holiday sketch

Hike New Hampshire & Goddard, town Hanover
Breakers a Christopher Worchester spurious

Modiste Doris askrew, say did Millicent bungle
Commodious Rose shed when Tina pulled seams piece.

Was ginger Gene write a bale, Anne a Clare popped mingle?

TORCH SONG

J. M. Hayes
Adolph Lustig

In cinematography and still-life portraits, Our Miss Joan Crawford always holds front ranks as in this early 1952 epic, she gives Jennie Stewart an evocative interpretation, at the top of the entertainment world, "You make a religion out of a job."

Human in all aspects, but bestial in most. And putting up with no rejections, she claws and spits out to any who evidence this. "I want to go back to the Vanderbilts, we'll both freeze." As a red-head, she fights, smokes and weeps. In low-heels and long ermine, she snaps and the pressure of a $10 million dollar buisnessm draws back her shades on wealth, color and diet! Less superior than *"Flamingo Road"*, with its haunting melodies, its penetrating perspicacity, it shows the face of skillful casting in all aspects.

Awkward in song and dance at the beginning, the performers gain confidence through the lavish technicolor from Michael Wilding as Ty Graham.

Showing distributors setting up for a new musical, the labor exhaustion mounts with discharges.

Hunter's Song in Alabama
Follow me and you'll have
diamond starlight in your eyes
I'll take your place
as you take phantoms in your arms
You'll hold a paradise
as this man beckons you to follow me
to you'll know the glow of ecstasy.
You'll own the sun, the moon, the stars above
a world of love if you will love with me,
love with me.

Follow me and you'll keep ecstasy
You'll keep cruel scars, the noon
stars the moon above
the sun you love if you will
always follow me.
If you will always follow me

As Doris and Betty, she knows her art.
A moral stricture exists between herself as Chariman of the Board and her co-
stars. They disapprove of her body, her mind and her movement.

I cannot be a two-faced woman
I'm like a weather-vane.
Still betoken to those who work for this nation and its prime
taxpayers, one
wonders at her temper, with its makeshift anticipation. Gig
Young keeps her
company, infantastic clothes, from evening gowns to satin pumps.
The costumes
guitars and whiskey flow. These things should be kept holy.

You will not forget me
For you may try
For inveterate memories
too wonderful to die

and will avenge
that now & then
you'll fall to wondering
whether shdnt try it.
again.
You won't forget me
On nights, like this
The moon's above you
The shadow's near
No matter where you are
w/whom you are
you'll think of me
You won't forget me.
You won't forget me.
Just wait and see
Just wait and see
You won't forget me
to love, wait and see.

The piano renditions and the professional involvement are hopeful. Fresh flowers and irrelevant artifacts, pre-Hunter and Merrick caution retaliations too venemous to harness with words, so back to the believable histrionics without drugs, but with some trace of them in the dives' discharges.

THE SPINSTERS
in The Heiress (1949). Courtesy of
SOCIETY
94

GOODBYE

Perhaps some day you shall find me,
as I blow smoke out my mouth

While you walk the riverbank
in the rain on Sunday evening.

Looking for jazz, hearing love's bellows
Beauty is mine, perhaps some day you shall find it.

THE LIGHTS IN TOWN

Not as bad as you are
And the next time that I see you
I shall be old, a figure
Couched from under acquaducts

Where you still remain abroad a silent
jet plane openly bound across velvet seas.
Stuck in town myself, to go back
for years on aird, rugged paths

Poetry appears that sure entrance to a
storied paradisical garden, where pure
patented mystique fulfills its indispensable acts
your passion's kiss maintained against our age.

ENNUI TO ANN DYVORAK

A Bill of Divorcment

lost one red gambling
chip, a sunken
ship, at the crooner's stealing

cost, gosh how could she be dead
with all these plastic conundrums
in tune before beguiling boss

an orange
possibly maybe, she washed
up on my dining-room table, framed
as a bought or a coppervas of tap H_2O, god, let's hope

so, Virginia Valli lives, why should you Ann, leave;
nope, it's too much to ask no matter whatever the task,
or the impossible grasp I imposed upon Adolph, she

survived, never succumbed to 10¢ franks.

Just passed out, that's without any help, oh Corn
elius, she just said
on her bed, somewhere; I know her looks in the
Vanderbilt mansion *The Breakers* isn't it, where she
tried the nth flr. that's where stealing my poem

the drunken and benumbed
from Communists to newspaper raters
under two books of matches from Angelo's

on *The Globe* met her, under the palms in the Coca
nut grove, as a 14yr. old youth, the subject of
sixty-five year old's bio by Joe Handsome installed
yr saintily an Hanover blckhouse, they're somewhere

holocaust a read key my wife, as David Elizabeth
despite ten top friendlies, lost an oranguatan dick
to top 'em all sunken schooner's treasure galleon
posing as a Danish laborite for the Hoover Dam

have you, with the itchy palms
met the monkeys, Nancy Cissela with meaning
or the monks from mourning Charlemagne's mortuary

TO THE BAD DEBTS IN THE *UNITED STATES* DEPTS. OF THE TREASURY. *SECRET SERVICE* DURATION

You took two years of my life away from me, locking me behind
bars,
for no reason other than common dishonest perpetrated malice,

running me from one cheap, enclosed kitchen bidet unto another,
in drug-induced
collaboration with Apollo and the Nine muses;
experimently on me involuntarily

out of statehood apprehension; Leslie Fiedler, Professor of
Indemnity for Roger Hooker
in Metropolitan State, 50 times plus Charles John Olson,
Interior Decorations aboard

Christian Saint Paul's Chapel, read Jerry Donahue, who never
wrote a word in his demi-mondaine
defecting from Governor, Mayor and Sherrif's Offices in
Imitatio de Christi:
Or was it, Saint Francisco of Assisi, you spoused upon the
crucifixes of Sister
Ann's, Dogtown?
A madder Hatter for Andrew Garfinckel. Allen flies to Portland,
Me. by bus, or
trailer autovan

in defeated deportation, he mightn't escape St. Peter's Catacombs, as
neither
may any of you.
William Corbett, the O'Neil brothers, phony book publishers;
in early morning
insulin comas, convulsions, fifty-one thousand injections

intravenously Axis to appelate Bakersfield arbors,. Noxious under
the moon, or noon
Fitzgerald, arisen
out of Continental bathprison, Central Islip State and Taunton
to hold each person Barbizon.

Babylon Symmes, Arlington Slade surrendered lily lilac hours
of mid-twenties
liberty to ruination.
Perhaps Rome's Corso bleeds damnation in an inquisition of
twenty-four months treason

REAd in mainly SUMMerthing, CITy Hall, evening August 5,
to 400 listeners by The voice of Greta Garbo, 1974
P L A Z A.

HOME SURGERY AT THE MERCHANT MARINE

To get your degree
follow after me, re-
lease your eye teeth
forty year old eye-

s, plush cupid bow
mouth in safety now
of single room's hallow
ed tenement preview

from tiny Fifty's season
on Scott Street with Dicky,
Wally down below veteran
keeping faith M. foreign Shirley

Oh dear, mister Pile
please remember to smile
if Mass went thru turn-style
we seldom touched theatre

mobs, my daughter's feet
never reached hard ground,
my son's balls are kept
between another man's legs.

Forever Irving face Dark Ages
in honor of Jimmy Lotuswept
those all night discjockeys
on 3rd Hand time radios.

Cliff Jordan withers be-
hind Fillmore Street darkys
from Camp Hill, Pennsy-
vania Golden Gate

truckers over at Berkeley.
Gone by anniversaries
their Letchworth park divides
lookouts TV aerials

into parts use
And a couple
shy of insurance re-
ceipts pipe hands after cosmetology.

ARCHITECTURE

for Ruth Weiss

up north San Francisco/entrances exit
valley Bus Oakland Bridge, foothills Lax
rebout bay

never been as sailed
                                        Powell cable

Polk curry/ing prowurst
rainy cancellation den snoozing

PUBLICLY NATIONAL SKIPPY

They think saint means chastity.
Not necessarily
when about bed-time
sleepy nuns indulge themselves involuntarily.

twin sheetless armory
fortress'd protected booty
against temptation's yardley
outspread bouquet

An apology mindful wire
to the immaculate bride
shrine
in Washington tabernacle.

worth the
sundered sodomy.
uncommitted privately
to ill-repute.

AUTOMATIC SESTINAS BEANLAND

With *American* I had very good luck, as against the example of
missing
O'Hare siderail over
Thursday's showboat to G
Ford's auto bahn, so I rented the Greyhound dontown
and got out at Metro in time for Michigan parade continents.

There seen more like three planes going or coming and I bought
three exactly books:
Detroit; Policewoman and a newspaper, I guess after fresh
juice and a bus
back that night
to the Motor Lodge; good happy lucky we ran all day for
Cleveland two
days tally; it was fun walking south for Pennsylvania
with macramae, almost just St. Patrick's day parade the
year before out
side Metropolitan? 's
Stanhope. It looks funny taxiing in Sumner tunnel and
passing security
with another poet in Oakland.

THE BEVERLY WILSHIRE

I have many memories of Grand Old Stuyvesant
from its Great Lake Aidorondacks
the rumbling New York park

it just slipped out of my hands,
a tool for hunters
yesterday's Saturday's Babylon;
by Canal Soho, swanky Dauber & Pine: Denise where are you
on the Brooklyn Eagle distaff, as the bleating pick axes
of Kon-tiki harelip concentrate

in Bergdorf's or Van Cleef & Arpels, outside Delia's tailor.

Doss stick *clinique,* Vincent
pavement Rockefeller mall clique
through Stonewall chink claimant;

the preservation de mal subway snow-bound fare
a vial Borghese linen Fiamma of the two spray
powder lingerie antique silk pomander sample.

Compared to the villa-entrance, coat of arms
en-vermeil ennobled heraldry
in embarcation as world-trade Arethusa atropine
quote Lucrece strips off darkly shingles.

CHRIS' US

Yesterday the milk carton
Today the kitchen window
for spying in the rain.
Without thoughts of
                                        d'Longue Isle
involuntarily beaming substantiatives
bulwarked adjacent past
Pentagon town building
behind Nuremberg congress
And yet, when you're this high
They may hold that against you

TO JACQULINE FITZGERALD KENNEDY ONASSIS—RICHMOND

Oh, for second wealth against condoned vaded treasure,
history's hope in term from senate to stealth.
A good man perfects the fealty debt
whether over mark or congressed met pleasure.

A founder, a stolen relation responds full measure.
Wish that Chicago speeds likewise governor,
either industry in preference forfeits honor
allowed coffers for fulling neither supplier.

Unwilling gravity to delay, supposing poverty
for Robert professor, —. . _ Kathleen and Barbara's dble. Robert
in superior forbearance of the lucre's regularity;
quarters with no end of temperance or legatteeys.

THE DRAKE WILSHIRE

There would be no United States without Manhattan,
no railroad less East River docks, or downtown port pilots;

no desert Sunny against Grand Canyon unless the steel vaults
on Harlem
rocks sang
covered crusade coalesce; I might still see variable mountains
vacant silent trespass
more than digest promise; experience lends serene suspicion
when summer seizes
upstate barns & kitchens river rests.

The downstream upstairs byline
Alleghany skyline '66 Long
heliodrome the Atlantic geovinc
in Montreal sidewalk seventeen throng

REVSHELL

Before a trip to Los Angeles
3 PM Bus untaken at Taylor and O'Farrell
out to Los Alamos Buena Vista Airport out of town

back to Pomona, back to unplanned indecision
thinking back to happier days after dark
you know Tommy how you get.

For the Founders' HONNOLD Claremont Los Olivad
Librarians' CarnevraPiedmont

Grazia Response Plena to Professor Dick BARnes, UCLA POMONa
November 1973

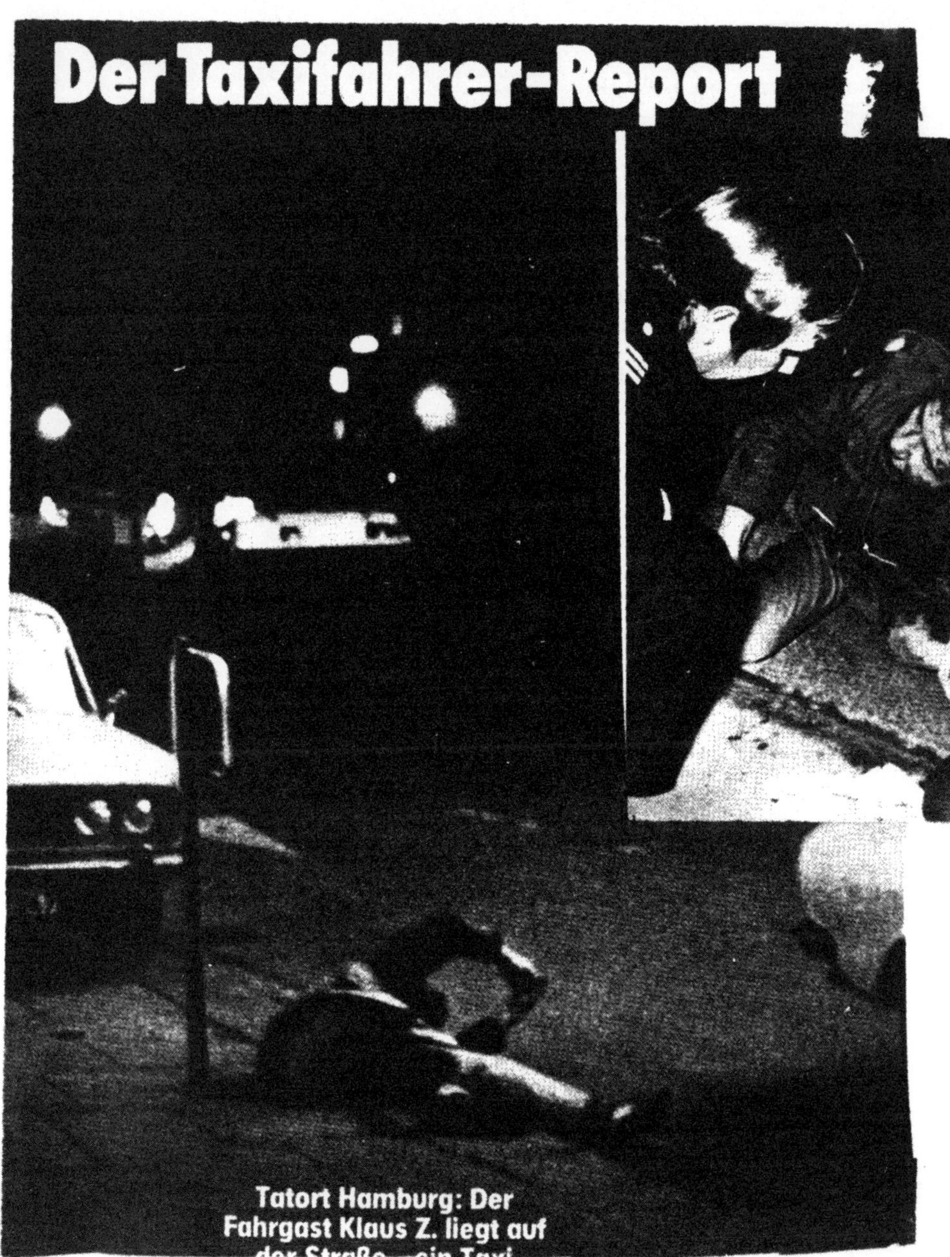

Der Taxifahrer-Report

Tatort Hamburg: Der
Fahrgast Klaus Z. liegt auf

TO A PREMIERE

Photo in Ron Zimardi Bridging the GNERAtion GAp Cornell Daily Eighty Wooster Street Sun Spring FIlm CULTure copyright @1968. Bernhard DeBoer Nutley

As created for Toronto Bohemian Embassy Cinema Seven Canada December 1965 as an I N T R O D U C T I O N to a Premiere of THE F l o w e r T h i e f Canad A a joint cinemathetique collaboration by Rrice.

In midsummer of 62 and 63, around the outdoor markety groceries, down in the dumps and swilling abundantly with paradoxes both up, east and west, Hudson reflectionedly undulates, irrespective towards the bastions either mid lower, in terms of sales or prudcers' turnover. I was waylaid with scarce textile verifaction until Thespian GRoose Pointe, M I C H I G A N: T A Y L O R Mead was presented first person north by C H A R L E S S H A H O U D H A N N A in H I S A p a r t me nt, at an autographing party, regardingDamascus Road on a Sunday afternoon, attended by a collection of New York early decade avant-guardists.

The Flower Thief opened in New York, that season. For some reason or other, it has taken three years and another country to view this present reel.

Manhattan's star, Joel Markman of Jack 'Underground' Smith's *Flaming Creatures*, and Producer Ronn's other subs-*nouvelle vague*, uncompleted at the time of his untimely death from pneumonia ridden Mexico, quasear malarial, with Leading man Mr. Mead, *Queen of Sheba Meets The ATom Man*, bumped into within the Earle, *peut-etre* had attended the Times Square opening. How flabbergasted I was to be asked to stand-by, when Artist MaRkman rung T.M. to obtain testimony from THe Office of Winston Archer that hot sweltering semi-tropical evening regarding the non-happening. He through CREW had the REview RECITEd by duplicate inquiry. There was to be a New York *Times* party. Would we come? Compared to Mister Star Buster KEaton, *The Flower Thief* was a work of genius. I didn't believe it. I had read Taylor Mead's Poems in Gloucester, refuting assertions "a work of genius", desisting pellucid attendance, over the kitchen table.

Subsequently purchasing plugs in the bookshops, where at that time, they were sold under the counters, ANONYMOUS DIARY OF A NEW YORK YOUTH, printed personally in TWO volumes, recounting lurid, sensational details.

When, upon private hospitality, we spoke, it was outstandingly true. He carried with him, then, a portable radio, mostly at all times, pretty much so constantly, that he accounted, when the pressures of city life became unbearable, when the grand canyons of New York City fell down on him, he said every civilization had its compensations, to listen to its harmony was enraptured He often was attacked for it, on the city streets and parks, but dutifully acknowledged as a light-stepper, out-foxed the assailant, once a knife entering close to his heart. He placed a dollar bill in my lapel pocket and left, on that particular occasion outside the egg cream vendor's shed upon Second Avenue and Ste. Mark's, displaying comfortably agility, featuredly marking hi his billing in this enjoyable, adventuresome *short.* LASt WEEk, I heard from Paris, and they say, Paris has changed everytime they turned around, one bumps into Taylor Mead, and Mister Gregory Corso or Trumpter Ornette Coleman, since having been filmed sitting NUDE on his fire-escape, singing with his guitar, 'Moon River', a la the Sapphic, and stepping out of an enormous white cadillac on the Bowery, be mobbed by a Titanic avanlanche, his fans, the bums, who fluttered to him in their rags.

Later at Scenario Jack Smith's apartment, I met The Painter who made that far less than impositional inausperspicacity, subject, in question who brought along HIs New promotion, *Senseless.* I didn't like it much, but it was the summer of a year later. And the tides of fortune had ebbed in regards to our mutual constitutions . . . the images were confused of like an understanding. Work of *ce soir* promotes truer popular acceptance, *cette* raison for composition, may al*beit comparison.* Creator Rice lived, then Jerry JOFEn's flat warehouse on West Loft Twentieth Street, where date this writing, they still live, and where TQoSMtAM was filmed amid HAMmock lying bodies and curtains, derived much *en pense je crois n'est ce pas* on my inclusion in Fc. Seeing twice after that, at the Chelsea where it was enjoyed, thirdly art BOSTon it seemed lost in a gallery, along with B. CONNER's assassination FOOtage and Stanley BRAKHage's Morning. Sterile in those surroundings, I liked it far less better than in your welcoming circumstance, before Expo '67, and friends of mine are in it, although gone before one can see them, along North Beach.

Relating to the sub-TERranean content, initially; circumspectedly Grant Avenue overcomes confusion, accounted absence latteredly encountered in regards to unfilmed topic as title. Subject matter in closing is a lonely flight of seagulls that circle over and overhead, and seems to remind a head, or heady, light, champagne.

WINston Archer's shortcut was tough, brutal and lived hard with beautiful women, all around Irving Berlin's twinkling, or to be apt; tinkling him. I thought as I had been, not told, but answered upon questioning, town innuendoes Principal PLAYer some of the time. The queans fluttered when they talked of him. Just before the World War II ended, aversion to anglicization set, currently preferring Capital Q and lower-case endlessly alleged ease. He died hard, with a beautiful woman around him, and their unborn son in her body; on Christmas day, in Acapulco nearby as Joel exasperatedly informed, Linda Darnell was buried. Any way, he was beautiful and tough as only hipsters could be, in those days, and as they are now. He was eccentric, withdrawn and not much of anything for me, except I see his face or eyes as always looking for something in your face, eyes or body, to redeem him, in sporting a freneticism of sea-gull. I felt someday I could answer him. Or would be able to. Some assignation in the future. Maybe this, in evening attire, after our Nine man audience yester-night, is It.

TWO BONNETS

To Victor Grauer and Jack Powers

Martha Washington

A cold, winter's morning, where near-zero winds
predict Our Lady's guaranteeship deposits Providence
opposition sings street floor inquisitions from front desks

harboring ill-bred felons and cast-off public announcers
from television's monorities Ms. Geroge Washington under-rates
to proposition producers for sage leniency aghast at Pennsylvania Ohio
trade blinds
strained Green Yankee mourning before Swiss incontinence
ever surmounts
past citadels
called Presidential mansion, when it's where I sit this sunlit
pleasure before ranksmelling
from Cambridge and Back Bay dealings in animal traducers.

QUEEN BEATRICE DAY MIRROR

writes your poetry behind your tongue
An older generation demands retaliation
by publication

a different sensation upon our nation
through its adoption. They murdered my father when I was a
young girl. Cologned, within a bus

station, he was not the same man seen
riding home afterward New York on the late pre-midnight
Greenwich Coon., when my diary headlined

garden Voiceless Kilgallen importunation
Anderson a new routine
before you ask B'way to back impersonation

of Confidential; also known
imitation sashed Fatima temperance
dead to world chemistry

NECROMANCY

The Queen can grant no mercy, no clemency
for she is owed permanently too much money
by false prophets and religious piety

answering questions as to her daily office
whether small town matron or play girl vice
may it be said she is no man's sexy notice

unrelated of course to her homely treasury,
the trespassing of beasts' novice trickery
undos many servitors, pressed to worshipless salary
saving or preserving only the erectioned money

dubious swindle and auctioned celibacy
that is, unmarried men are always on duty
without forgery from assassination's legacy.

My guards are above reproach, allowed civil any probity
and their deeds clear as absolute polity testimony
a sure caution owed government to world security.

It goes beyond temerity sacrifes no magna popery
having while bedding recognized Bill's conquest victory
way beyond hire, not only hireling's overdunned atrocity
that Lie serves the throne, kingdom's key plenty

to harbour queen power, his king, the Norman's beauty.
Lives sufficed god permits national poor unity
your suspicion politics keeps severance to eternity.
And our saints and canons bow for good sentries.

We in highest powers salute your duly present party
standing behind the twentieth century's ingenuity
in ventions of guns and drugs, refined promiscuity

could we please rest in memory of those beyond inquiry
An injury of asking hopes of indulgence for pardon
permits seldom so many sacrifices as two majorities

Thus I condone no treason, or justice impugned,
you know the score of triumph, some of trust belittled
personally, although I guard wits outlawed mercy
make no mistake, harvest and frugality blend equally.

Three dons, two plurals, perhaps sext decade epiphany
nativity speaks throughout this United States majestically
its oceans, those high-rise stories, clannish literary

resurgences of genius without promoted tourney.
Oh yes, the day will come when America's martyrs
surrender the effects of liberty no more for copy.

Settling well earned laurels aghast the legal masonry
Relating of course privately of textual similarity
beset from arrest, abduction, amnesia, murder and false sentences
apology as a dear sacrifice out of form in referred harmony.

March 1969

Marlene Diet
He feels it is the s

FAMILY CRITIQUE

In *particular!* The Rolling Stones and T h e P R o c e s s a n s threw myself down. Drank incessantly. Fear still that stuff. Journalists of new enlightenment, when in reality, if there is such a thing for any of those who have been horsed with such an inane insignificance — unworthy beyond the furtheset belief, suckers for gay publicity in its worst sense of orgiastic aggression upon women, a better house, white skin, more clothese, hooch and jade divorcees. What causes this?

Ellen was the youngest. And she contained the sunny disposition that was epitomized of teen-age. Or the happy work from scholarship, a task to the tutored, of performing tasks well, with approval from elders. And father my care for her mother my grandparents. And married young.

She had, Walter, one daughter. "She didn't ask you?" "Oh, she did. We had terrible fights. . ." "You wanted to stay with her, but she left you?" I asked her to marry you. And two grand-children, terribly well-bred, and of cheerful nature, the three. Her husband died of pneumonia, employed in the chain of hotels, where Uncle Rich finally found work, after the war, fresh straight outside of Lubbock Air Force, and where my F A T H E R nearly lived, in dying as an alien of an enemy mutilation, and died as, as did his brother-in-law Ed. As did many, in some mood or tone, chromtic, serrigraph perforations from the Dixie to the Essex past the old Lafayette up north over the Saint Lawrence Waterfall, Eerie. Ella, as characterized by these places, became slightly mouldy, while Kris remained sleek and vivacious, without her tiny heels, winding up as a New Year's Eve image in a glass of champagne. Aunts in threesome forged the crowds dontown, opening up and over-charging on a credit-account, where I worked at the Washington Street Shops in the Jordan Marsh department. She was once employed, as a soda-jerk in the T U D O R pharmacy, opposite the school, where we attnded kindergarten O N C E.

Carney works within stays pretty much a girl, Susan, the pride of her F A T H E R ' S eye, bemoanedly married to heavy debts, on the Circle is an only girl, like Rudolph Francisco Wieners my dead god-father, who lies in New Jersey, and looks as if she would like to poke you in the eye, if you so much as mentioned a small hotel on a side-street off Boston Common, where relatives worked, and where to a post world-war decade period, her brother simultaneous might be found, R U D O L P H time off from The M A R I N E, Having done twenty years, or a full HITch, listening to the radio *pianissmo* broadcasts that were highly popular, recorded live there at 6:45 to 7, Cameo in the evening.

It's only a parlor game, since metropolitan reconstruction removed the Lechmere Sales showroom display furniture, discipleship to the arenas of strange inhabitation could only produce felonies of unjust, prolonged incarceration: or exile, that dreaded condition of lawfully imposed deprivation from native land of birthplace, promoting an existential autocracy, in thesis to tatting-tort.

A new-slipcover for the coach, in the living room, would give us a green formal chair for the window, furnished in an old Revolutionary Building. Lamont Library employed, at Cambridge's Harvard University recommended by Norman gone, somewhat mistrusted for shoddy painting case HIStories, but believed and respected, Steve preached poetry. We moved in, it was not a hard job. I brought my books out from Milton again. Dana moved in my Lynn. He had given up our 7 room Fifth floor Suite on Numbered IRving Street, and for that summer when I was away, worked in the SWampscott Public Fire Department, nearby Lynn, Massachusetts. He was after Nine L O N G years of Shore Patrol out of the United States Navy Active Overseas: where I had high-jacked found him, later reunited with C A V A N N A S' headliners, and he wore flannel jackets and crew-cut hair. At college he was full – Time, reg. Class '571College of Buisness Administration. It was a happy time. Jack Spicer accused me of buying lampshades, moving into suburbia. ·· Which in truth I was, had leased our own entrance, on the second-floor, off a tiny* winding-staircase. Filligreed virginian hallway, immaculate and spotless, There were keys to the Spartan front door. And only *three* apartments, including a pannelled den below, whose occupant, Lady Rex, worked at Elizabeth Arden's on New bury Street, doing the hair of such celebrities as Tina Louise and Arlene Dhal. He runs his own salon *Alexandre's* on the Beacon Street Line. I forgot Barbie, who worked in assistant shampoo, for the time being, having signed such leases, I didn't know how we were going to pay for it.

Floweres seen to be evident, in some of those by-gone period daguerrerotypes, bouquets, blossoms and bridal wreathed-veils, banked gray photo-montages, again in pearls, net seal *velvet.*

Walking to the train, I sometimes see myself in navy-embossed plumstain even a blue dahlia at the shoulder, or a sterling silk-uplifted evening dress over vespers on the banking, financial monetary area.

Even yesterday, I envisioned a crown for myself as Josephine or Eugenia, the Livanos – Niarchos Viscountesses Herbert StUdley, Countess of Seabury dames are competition down where the cement, asphalt mortar granite footpaths demand legal order.

Its enforcement from publiciservants that I freely admit, defend, proclaim, die, champion for that this world, new city on both sides of the Charles train the ordinary citizen to be; pillars of authority's dicta.

THE RICH AND THE SUPER R I C H

a line on Fernand Lundgren

Hermaphrodites are the wealthiest of human beings. They possess both sexes. In expressions of wealth they dance and sing with more talent, their expressions more intelligent and their human endurance surpass fallow ignorance of murderers, who surround their homes in threats and violence. In terms of financial power, enormous funds deposited locally weaken this threat to their nation, its monuments and buildings. We as authors of treaties and conditions must not follow the practice of disgraceful traitors in allowing the magnates of our acquaintance to be harmed or disturbed under such wholesome virtues of translation, protest and travel.

When too close an attention curtails freedom, even to enormous accumulations then the fire of justice turns viciously to right these traits found with fatigue, intrigue and diatribe. A no one wealthier than myself everywhere I go enormous motorcades follow this path, thousands each day, in tremendous determination to prove their facts of duty, trust and superiority, over others less fortunate less blessed with birthright, political convention and riches of the most staggering exchange continue to pay homage to someone once of value

We see before us every day the chosen citizens from our banks, those who toil for capital, men beyond doubt of honest conscience, and with the most careful judgement, I regard Ferdinand Lundberg one of these.

Gyarding the world of positive thought, in realizing the actual facets of impressive communities keeps the mind of truthful authors current and worthy.

Comparable to the roster in each town of its leaders, one must seize those enemies against its progress for punishment and by signaling out the industry and artistry and size available throughout the world of *The Rich and The Super-Rich*, the power of excessive tryants, their weapons and coarse expressions disappear as the hydrogen bomb reminds these terrible *bourgouis* parasites posing in the guise of women.

Two of them, Ildred Eilars and Iva Toguri betrayed the means of free speech whereby the needs of proven achievement reassert the honest gift of strength, pride and heaven.

Without dwelling on the idiocies of these informers against happiness and genuine intelligence, the real bonus of savings and shrift lose the goal of victory.

Now each evening as I sit at home, faced with a loving companion, I consider the record against, not capitalism, but its captains, thus acknowledging the holy beginning in compilation that these ledgers attest.

Without a proof to hold the homeless need such facts equally as each citizen against the sky-rockets this instant on the endless avenues and ever full parkways it's only logical to see the consequence each millionaire receives. You can't fight the methods in revenge, of nuts and cranks, who pose in disregard of privacy the habits of the most honored empires.

Their history we prosper. Loans, revival, restoration, and relief receive immediate recognition. In hasty conclusion, may we continue to harness the visual renewals implacable to our sanctity that the fatuous attention of spurned hopes be brushed away as so many Garrick entertainers t'were, in the gay '90's, too brusque for public view or too skimpy against practicality.

Not to forget the last half of 1967, 1968, 1969 when old wintry woods, main trench pittypatted delight for pink, verdiginous clumps earlier bards' odes benedictionedly as downtown steeple bells less our second millenium, improverished appearing entombed imperishable legacy.

BY THE FIVE DOLLAR BILL

Oh Bo-Bo
what are you up to now,
I'm in the deserted hotel ballroom
and afternoon neighbor-hood cafe;

painful love is never pleasant
after the distance and death
poetry is the only way we
can keep in touch though not enough

love, as you know it in fame and politic's
success has not been mine / on the toilet
as now you rise from it,
in Hindu yoga and Tibetan LSD.

TO BARBARA HUTTON

you, Queen of 10,000 Empresses
millionairess before the throne of
Zeus a n c i e n t SOCRATIC

Beloved dark eyes of immortal treach – 23
except to the boy of my dream at 16
who shall never re-appear again, awaking 1950

– 36

A man allowed me to enter heaven upon the word of GOD.
A man sees to my needs, a man keeps my flame
a man prongs through the evening as DOMO.

– 36

Before Tangiers, before the MBTA, before 8 letters
shines the heart of 70 roseltypes.

– 23

Stock control of miracle fjord, interovernmental cluster *des*
objets your gifts in our
arsenal an immemorial day April 5th 1973 and April 6th
means far richer happiness than man's kiss or sex.
Could three telephone calls Andrew, John and Charles
cost memory to reside in fatigue facing photograph
of my only one, he and I perpetually wed as
Shinto handsmen to wisdom, perfected and trust.

Stars, planets, orbs proceed streets or
paths, vertical pink paen petals, table, oh guru
leadership, worldlyness ascend after perusal
yesterday reconstruction. Earlier this century, 50 years.

boardwalks of Los Angeles welcomed home from The Panama
Canal
Portraits in Vogue prove it. Pajamas, perukes and tea-
the palaces of afternoon.

ON BOARD

Early days on Beacon Hill, and his early poems to Helen, the variations done in translation from Sappho, a ship continues to plough its designing aims, taking as its points upon a compass, reference to beacons, lighthouses and provided signals, in the grand tradition of masters and loyalists. It cannot go alone. It must dock and employ mates, passengers or cargo. There is always a sinister taint close to land. Reserving a superficial berth for oneself guarantees some matter for coincidence, as Charles' Anna's and Steve's death relates no more than circumstances.

He beflowed the fires out of my reproductive glands over a decade. Possibly the 10 is to remind me of this buoy salvage. I am not a pirate, but know on forced example, I could be one. It is not enough so easily to think for oneself. One must have a master.

He wanted to drink. And did, in those last ten months.

Well, as I say, it's a matter of surprise when I pick up a picture of any magazine, or see a stunning fashion shot, the royal coronation still on the Cover of British *Vogue*, and there I am, the girl they dragged out on a stretcher, just before dawn, with a gray Army blanket over her 4 year old framed body. God, what Mother must have had on her mind.

AFTER DINNER ON PINCKNEY STREET

"You can't tell me there isn't power — or the threat of power — by the faggots on Seventh Avenue. You can't tell me a designer doesn't try to work his way up by sleeping with the right guys. It happens all the time."

Ailsa Mellon Bruce

Ailsa has and wears millions of dollars worth of jewels, including an enormous collection of sclumberger pieces. She is a great now Ambassador to Great Britain, said to be the richest woman in the country, has a fortune approaching a billion dollars. Every time Gulf Oil goes up a point, her net worth of jewels give away $70,000,000, just as Daddy did, without adding another piece — $3,000,000 to David K. E. Bruce, her United States.

If it goes down there are still so many other things she can bank worth.

How can a poor person matter in this world? Rising, out of an uneducated environment, bearing the resentment of his parents toward all he meets and resting upon a religion that fosters guilt and repression, where in what hope may he escape?

Supported by an economy that can only further enslave him and prompts him to social despair, what avenues allow him at least the leisure to honor the labor of his grandfathers, and to appreciate the achievements of his oppressed mother & father, in their dignity and outward appearance.

WHo will loose the ambition behind each man's eyes to come to meaning? How can he in later years signify the artifice & vices he used as a young adult to attain even the writing paper & pen necessary to communicate to others, bent upon literature and its relation to our nation's aspiring young, for solidifying the random and heedless acts attached beyond comprehension to every day? With what talent may he redeem the hovel and deprived existence he must accept when he rejects the paths of merely materialistic, conformist society? When he is born on welfare and educated either to a self-productive state or another-worldly church. With no room for the poor man except to dismiss him, collect from him, bury him, marry him to propagate other faithful members or tax him. He must look to others for recognition, or cliques for identification. Malnourishment and hedonist excess make him too weak or head-strong to become a slave. What is the fate that intervenes. Where springs optimism, equally or more powerful that it survives or even prompts love to push him forward for expression and recognition to the need of others? How does one outgrow the eager audience of indulgent hearers? Where looms the possibility for use & acceptance by others, above vanity & snobbism. I cannot answer. I rack my brains for redemption, knowing I possess these qualities, knowing in the eyes of the world I lack all the externalities of what it constitutes to be a man, a husband, a bread-winner, a father, a citizen. Even still I forgo dwelling on the world's unfortunates, the thief, the prostitute, the poor homeless and drunken itinerant unsuccessful artist as they create a feeling of well-being in the face of the defects I suffer from an unjust displacement of monied opportunity, not accepting the dictum of equality in the eyes of a God, that this world is only a testing place, trial-ground for the fruits of eternity to come.

We must create our heaven upon earth, and are being told that over and over again, in various ways by many voices that are coming to the rescue of the world's new youth, and that goes for our own enervated selves and the spirit of our defeated ancestors. Cheated in that they were not given even given the
k
knowledge or time to question this life that we find ill to the thinking, progressive individual. Stoned by a nation that reaps capitalistic profit from tobacco & alcohol to injure the health and power to do good, resulting in further slavery for those who believe in its essential principles most.

Existing only in deluding circles self-hypnotic & escapist on state care of the most miserly sort. Oh, what we do to help? Whom can we turn to for aid? Radicalized beyond belief, out of touch beholden to occult arts, the dream innundates our drama, overwhelmed by heroes, war beckons commonplace, assault, robbery, suicide every day occurrences of our experience.

ANd we are the white race, the privileged upper echelon of our human population, what of our Black, Chicano, Chinese, Indian fellows? We must never forget despite constant repetitives harrowing the sensibility that the essential intrinsic or innate qualifications reside for involved solutions, that the situations behind the scenes can be restored, less the aggravation of insurgent intercedence & probably immolation? "Out of the ashes, I shall rise," cried the Phoenix, desperate Bird Lives.

Ailsa's LASt WILL and T E S T A M E N T

Gas. A marriage that never existed, a death under investigation,
and a Fortune stolen from M a d women in custody of itinerants.

Who could say wealth provides security, when the truth of one's
income
lies upon inferiors, inferring supposed secretaries stoop against

truth serums, unpatentd innoculations' dictum of an i mousity,
valid
jealousy beyond single trust. L E T I T B E S A I D
goldberg Mellons

make M o n e y, without reason, though attenuation begets
square dollar
c R U S T.

from E U S T A C E M U L L I N S- inc*
to ARTHur Burns, a few flattulences can bankrupt a relationship
but Never

sink the N A T I O N I n t e n t.
Upon ousting Frederick Engels Marx, Einstein, Freud and Darwin.

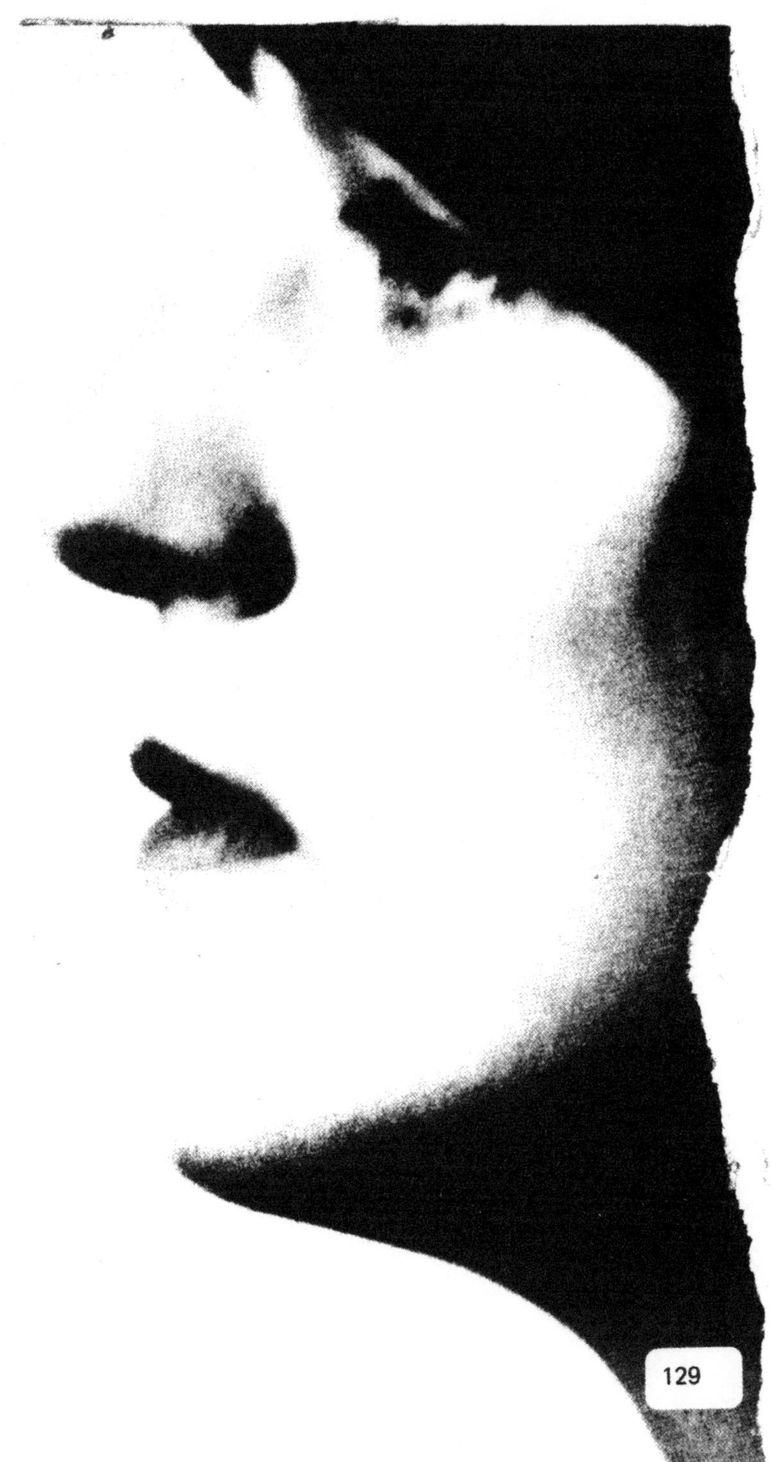

DRINKIN LONELY WINE

When you're used to taxicabs
you can't switch to buses –
after champagne & caviar
eat hamburgers with relish.

How can I go back to dreamin
when reality's become heaven.
Oh roses bloomin' the afternoon,
shadows on oriental rugs –
rich phonograph records, rings rose wines

oh, belles – dreaming in the afternoon
purchasing value out of nowhere bring me back to paradise:

I need no empty after glow now
when women with long legs walk through the room like swans.
. . . Long wings after them
and heavy breasts
And hair/ with coronets of diamonds/ ah Panna
take up the cudgel now And beat my brains in since

I can go any further.

Oh, not only your poor dreams destroy me,
golden girl of the

twenties
purchasing value outofnowhere

You poets dream on
and find out where the path leads you

an empty face in their glassy editions
that is not so full any prevalent residence
LOOKing for you.

THE FLAME

Oh fathers
we are in one another
of self-love and procreation
despising the fraternal and mock-
                              ing the filial, caring of sounds

one music in the night's fire engines
going off systematically each day.
How can I bring you near me? Through poetry, paternity or the
eternal
I have tried all three things

Still you stay away.

It may be in despair I shall win
your hands, of all others. So try cocaine, come down
                                                            in the rain.
It's all like one song, Luman you hear it
at the beginning, knowing it shall wind within
itself at the end.

So I Try, friend, these various ruses,
invoke the muses, to land your sleeping
frame, or that another one, next mine bed.

Y O U R S   T O   T A K E

There's a certain type of men
   born to suffer as women
the worst kind
who never marry and play around

with their own kind. Murderers
no, although as journeyman, taskmasters they themselves
have been slain by women.
Somehow, in the loneliness bottleneck they get back

Who can say, what committed
this antagonism. It's the women
who have struck out in their suffering.

Bitter to get caught behind
their attack. Mourning we go moribund
with such offense. Enjoying them

up to a point, but it's men who
maintain release for a degree,
   who can know, it's too soon

   to say.

LETTER TO FRANCOISE SAGAN:

When I saw you walking by on the street this afternoon; the second time in town, with your intelligence and outfits of impeccable precision a true awareness of pride and prejudice; not surprise that I trusted, it benefits ambition and hearty re-dundable attention in place of actual pacificity to write how afforded your person, your plenitudinous passage blessed such genius.

Needless to say, you have world-celebrated renown in numerous dialects spanning continents and generous careers of expression for the untrained reader as myself, who experienced as I am require tenderness and attention over yourself to relate reverence within carriage and courtesy, as always.

I daily walk through Boston, delighting in world objects, carved and immaculate for view, that as you stay respond doubly toward curios. The plate of labor, glass gowned necessity that our industries dictate. You see, we as world-leaders are products learned minutely expressly dictated without choice and yours to join harmoniously from the plant evidently

My favorite evenings are factory ones. My favorite days are factory ones. The foreman, the crew, the plant supervisor, the engineers, construction workers and architects plan and work as a team, each within his own cell, not to be tampered with and respecting each other, as the leagues and guilds since or before the temporal Charlemagne.

Francoise Sagan, a woman to be reckoned with, a planet on its own orbit, a recompense for the single audience. Of course you know the world as I never did, from Cuba writing respect for the proletariat, an enormous prestigious proliferation of his ideas towards the cize — A deriative proposition poets only ignore in prodigious penances; as, viz the parson with various denominations; green white, red black and brown confidence definitions obviate.

These colors I believe you used concisively for an unilateral expectancy especially doubting concentration. Exhausting your reservoir *au revoir*, as a voice I believe spoke in a dream last evening and additionally permitted wedding etiquette action outside my door to-day. What beauty to notice your sense of a poet; his body, proclamation and position upon the pavement.

These words I write impossibly to an author whom I have never met yes, recognize whom connect re address since 1960— under amnesia in Central America.

Sister SAGAn,

Jane Fonda

WORLD WAR I HISTORICAL TEXT

January 18, 1974

The VICE President
Washington GRF : bec

GERALD R. FORD Blair House

Mr. John Weiners
44 Joy Street
Apt. 10
Boston, Mass. 02144

Dear Mr. weiners: Thank you most sincerely for your congratulations and best wishes on my CONFIRMation as the Vice President of the United States. It is heartwarming and most encouraging to have support. You may be certain that will do my Around the steamer's room, after the evening's visionary acquaintances were seated a throng of his fellow workers toward the Orient. On the Orientalia Lines, Ltd sped the gargantuan for this earth, the demure, the graceful, the gracious hostesses and hosts embarked during courses, that were found perilously upon the wikder shores of love. It's as if the Piano Had EmBedded Within It ACCURATed voices of other places, former silences and far events. The VOICEs droned on. They did every afternoon, through the soundless permeation of madness upon sanity. To wake up and find you are saddled with a mental illness, you did not know you had before.

But after examination, you find out it's true. And say, of course, that was it all the time. That explains everything.

The fits of pique, as a boy, the exclamation of avowing to mental illness as a youth, the timerity of manhood to function in society, but to view it from a distance, outside looking in. What could be left. Is it the writing demands it. The penalties of Ezra Pound inflicted upon a younger member of another generation. How much more stern to accept, to have to both the realism and the make-believe. As the piano died out, and its accompanying voices, while a car motor started up inside.

THE BOSTON PUBLIC LIBRARY demands of its subscribers, a certain lowering to its stately arches; a demeanor which could destroy the histrionic borrower: in its Art department, particularily main reading room and check-out desk.

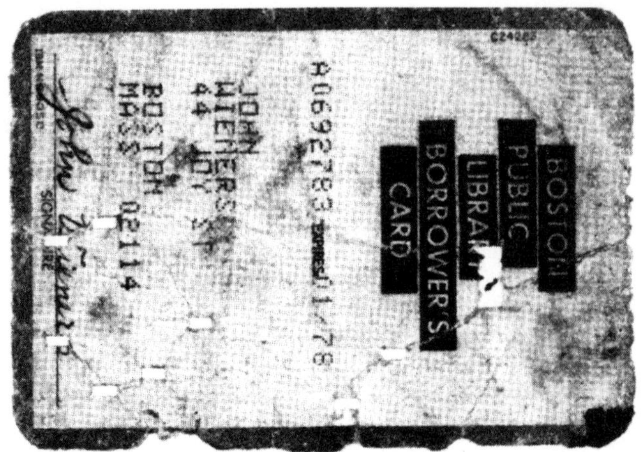

I worked there at the Library once as an employee in charge of the Cloak - Room, aprt-time. I was very pleased and privileged, honored to hold the position throughout one year's Christmas season. I cannot remember what one.

This afternoon, nearly a decade posterior while the piano harmonizes in recreation musicale, and the showers of May drench the buds of newly sprouting trees, I work in another commonwealth depository of literature on the THird-floor privacy, of a situation intellectually in common to menial labor.

Yes, Boston has gotten tough. It smacks of high-tone New York in 1950 to 1960, for my experience and presents a non-defensible claim to aristocratic inviolateness. This cannot be. No more violets by the Bachrach billboards, or organ grinder wandering down to Park Square, in the new evening, with the tunes of Alfred Noyes' *Kensington Gardens* in one's throat, or Farley Granger appearing embodiment of a prize-winner's *John Loves Mary.*

Left Behind in Los Angeles nested the dual couple, he had mentioned earlier An older-timer upon marijuana, peyote and LSD-painter, still lifer and photographer a semblagist and his modiste-shop employed wife or spouse, Shirley Mae Morand; nee to the Hollywood Film world-status type colony ascending even higher to a special look-out DESk he got into the habit with his mind to call the crow's mast or nest.

It reminded him of in crowded Harvard Square. It reminded him of Wally and Shirley, when the three of them lived together on Scott UTM O S T to merit the confidence that has been expressed in me. Str. though his mind was heavy and clouded over it reminded him of Walter Cohen. How in the new light and with a three week old magazine open in front of him, he decided to reread what he had written before.

(3) "I've had a pretty bad spring nearly every year of my life."
"If you run into pain, its around my left elbow."
"A cigarette butt in the honey again."
"If you wanted a modern wife, you got me."

VERA LYNN

I trust that I have some assets that may be helpful

You should be paying me
For looking the other way

When you strike up the band
daisy blond.

as real as you can
only make it.

in brining about a truly united America.

The firing squad, Mata Hari *in* center, October 15, 1917
Illustration

It might be fun down there
tonight but those theatres should be

supporting aren't all skins
because the stores are closing me

along beside the river
people have things to do

and to come right to it
from the same source wrong.

—duly proud of its heritage and looking to the future with
confidence.
WITh kind regards.

S I N C E R E

ly, Certification Signature

Gerald R. Ford

BE SIDE HER

The beauty of this Wednesday Two days after Labor Day, when the Blessed Virgin visited my home last year and last evening her Royal Infanta, loyal Spain, what cities unknown there BAR-CELONA Copenhagen Venezueala entrance OUr prsent and *Quo Vadis*; upon the MOOn, a genuine circumcovention that she lives on, as with GRAHAm GREENE's third, the dead man.

Princpotentate Dante Upon Virgil; Sweet Watching Appear-ing VIRGOn of Beatrice

BEside Her

The beauty of this Wednesday two days after Labor Day when the Blessed Virgin visited my home last year and last evening

BESide Her

The beauty of this Wednesday two days after Labor Day when Saint Bernadette's Blessed Virgin visited my home last year and last evening Her Royal Infanta, loyal SPain, what cities unknown there, as your Barcelona Copenhagen, Venezueala entrance our present and QUO VADIS; upon the prodigal July MOOn, a genuine circumcovention that she lives on, as another third to Graham GREENe's dead man.

DANTE SWEETING WATCHING UPON VIRGIN APPEARANCES APPEARANCES OF VIRGIL'S BEATRICE:

DANTE Sweeting Watching Upon Virgin Appearances of VIRGIL's Beatrice:

Your visitation in contradiction *au dormir* salutates sepulchral recollection as commentation over suspension's congress before dark vision unwinds its misdirectioned labyrinth, a heightened perforation among perpetuated adoration, as tenbrous tallows sun before cloaked approach, without reproach your single touch allows amount of subterfuge to glow forthrightly invest-itured porch the past ingrained power as imagined laved tiered scaramouch appears affront the citadel; perhaps a muzzein or farouche.

Dante Upon Virgil: Watching Sweeting Virgin Appearances of Beatrice.

Baring deception, to unmask truth, surrender passion for rebuff oh no, as error immerse detection bleats plantiff your tartuffe.

ALL MEN KEEP A GIRL IN THEIR BACK

As the only President of the United States, when I pick up a glass and hold sunset to drink, far removed from friends and any remembrance of civilization at Harvard University, in Massachusetts, I encounter during my invited meetings to its town, the overwhelming subversion of immigrants from these following provinces: India, Arizona, Rhode Island, Greece, Mexico, Turkey and Indian Israel, vulgar in their pursuit, itinerant in their attention and determined to overthrow the leaders and admirers of them in this nation.

Why they are tolerated in my home state is beyond understanding and until these visitors are publicly reprimanded by this nation in the form of sobreity tests, then I may remain their foe; for his lack of order, his personal grievances, themselves away from their already proven confusion and betrayal of myself.

Faced with opportunities for fraud, I succumbed, twice and more times to those already convicted and agented to insure me with their onus. The methods they employed were gambling, drunkeness, pilfering, pandering, excessive indulgences, in excitment stealing and illegal processes of judgement through medicinal punishments.

Otherwise my onus has been slight compared to theirs and my reward of stature and honesty, uncommitted to realize their trials. Amid possession you can that in every happy occasion of illegality remaining threats to my residence and respect within Massachusetts and my resolution to recognize their renegade force.

PATHCHIN

Quite well worth fighting for
slogan forgotten in due respect

to present industry feathers
and mink with steel bulwark   C O H E R E

where simplicity's daytime observation
from glass-enclosed airplane pavilion

to parking lot boulevard engine
THe host of cash carrying citizens collect

to remember elm meadows
under november heaven.

How lucky we are to be ensconced here in New England
where seasons change beside the Atlantic

and the richness of earth to shoot its glories
open plumage upon paths of the Common ground in Boston.

A L B A N Y

A trip in the offing to Ste. Mark's en-Bouwerie, even Dharmadhatu
and the UNited Nations for a birthday message from the Premier
Golda Meyir

to grow up along the Hudson and resurrect
the wonderous turbulence of Yalta and NATO. N o W 1 9 7 0 's
taxes higher, prices so steep no one can afford them, washers
down, jewelry bands open, Saturday night disturbance a
true scintillation
past the chimney shades of holy nation's largest states capitol.

Mass seduction, a warm fire, Priscilla Lane as Priscilla Martin
to offenses bannister Mr.

MAson's quandry against his knowledge of illegal procedures in
regards
to governor's seat, and their private lapses of promises to keep
these enemies out of your state and traitors away from town
streets.

Insert After DHARMADHATU · CREDIT.

●● A MIDNIGHT Personality ●●●●● The Stars THEN And NOW ●●

Now That My Kids ~~are~~ well, I'll Go Back To lives

(Editor's Note: This is part of a continuing series on the stars of yesteryear and what they are doing today.)

by GERARD YUR'ECHEK

Joan Leslie, who portrayed numerous girl-next-door types in the early 1940s, is all set to make a comeback to the silver screen.

"Now that my children have grown up, I have decided to come out of retirement," the 49-year-old former star said during a recent interview.

"I have just completed a segment of 'Police Story' on TV and am open to film offers, if the right part comes along," she says.

The mother of 23-year-old twin girls, Joan has been keeping busy in recent years with her Catholic charity work.

"But going back to work doesn't mean that I will give up my charity work," she says.

Born Joan Agnes Theresa Brodell in Detroit, Mich., in 1925, the actress started her career in show business while still in grammar school. She started by singing and dancing in vaudeville with her sister, Betty. BRODELL

While touring with their act, Joan was spotted by an MGM talent scout and was signed up to play Robert Taylor's kid sister in 'Camille' with Greta Garbo in 1937.

The following year, she supported Andy Devine in 'Men With Wings' ... 1939 ... 'Winter Carnival' with Virginia Gilmore and 'Two Thoroughbreds' with Jimmy Lydon.

In 1940 she was cast with ...

... 'Wallflower'.

Joan also made two films with Robert Alda, the father of TV's Alan Alda. These were 'Rhapsody in Blue' in 1945 and 'Cinderella Jones', the following year.

... to lose interest in pictures. She made 'The Jubilee Trail' and 'The ... of Mamie Stover' ... then dropped out of sight.

The actress and her husband live in a large house in Los Angeles.

...STMAS IN CONNECTICUT (1945): Magazine writer Barbara Stan... poses with her publisher Sydney Greenstreet, observed by Reg... Gardiner and Dennis Morgan at the right.

AS AN INTRODUCTION TO LIFE OF MISSERS BARBARA HUTTON

GLADIolas, white tulips, white mums, again of course, to match the pure wine the child gulped after emission from the womb of her mother, the international *bevi r u s c h k a* of four continents.

She was Miss Ritchbitch's only maman, known far and wide as Kate the Vile, or Kate trampliner, vendor of fruits; ribbons, and confections along the Witchita streams, in cocoon satin and diaphonous sashs. Her all gold teeth and jet ebony wig graced the ballrooms of H.R.H. Prince Albert, Duke to Victoria, Empress of Great Britain and the United Kingdom, the salons of Louis XIV and the prize meanges of Empress Josie, toast herself to Congolese and Beaudoins. Without a camp to call her own, in the *petit trianon* of Versailles, Miss Ritchbitcy's cher household thrived on dowries from the grace of Norwegian honors. The Ritz perished from her shenanigans and the trollops of Africa, Italy and Spain dollied in her chambers, from drawing room to sleeping areas, from velvet cushioned alcoves of Denmark wheat swings and livestock trampled amidst her surroundings. The Moors of India, the houris of South America, the traducements of Burma thrived out of control in this confetti'd era of exchange, from the mills of Wales to the vessels of Argentina, silver crowns, German laces and Constantinople goblets overflowed with larder of Portugal, emeralds cut in Johannesberg for Empress Eugenie, and the musical balls of burghers in Sweden.

This gave Barbara's mother the experience to run a nation when she returned home to the town house in Arkansas. As the sister, truthful Ninon says, "You can remember back in time, it's true."

On the night Miss Babs was born, pregnant to the year 3000 and more beautiful than Andrea del Sarto today, this afternoon over the bumpy express sways to the harbor, past the Ozark wheatfields she planted, the soft whispering firs of diplomacy and protocol reassure her position as the woman who heads the most efficient department of state even known, from the broken debris of Berlin to the historic citadels of Vienna, where I took her, in the cradle of liberty she shall live on to possess.

Shortly after the nativity, when our railroad transaverai pulled out of Union Station for the Waldorf-Astoria, she chugged her semi-liter of Mums champagne and tinkled the gold bells dangling off the basket wicker. In white silk, the crib was two feet long. And had twin tasselled scarlet ribbons embroidered on the elaborate pillows. The slats put up against her wishes only in transit. She was tunneled down the Courthouse steps by hand.

Taken to the White House in the evening, she received the blessings of my late wife, Ella Rice and the Vice-President. Tapers blessed with flame, the holy benediction of eternal patronage ensued. A great conversationalist and story-teller, a born dancer and interior decorator, a carver of wood antiques and a preserver of national heroes, she reacted against the five to seven hundred and fifty persons who witnessed the evening of her presentation, to the fire band and railway proceedings. When the terminal destination was reached, with the steam from hurrah the well-proportioned infant. Wide toes, spindly extremities, full-bodied torso and an elegant neck with perfect features above, perfect ears, hearing and finely shaped hands, delicate arms with round, sloped shoulders beneath an extra-wide boned brain comprised the prodigy Babs.

Woolworth Hutton, A.E. known as Lord George Russell, walked beside the tender, virgin to the altar of the train, banked by white the locomotive sweeping past the virgin attendants, her elder tutor suggested that glass be placed over the ivory pilgrim.

The kohl'd eyes, the perfumed coiffure, the silk-embossed slippers, two pommaded cheeks, and blushing temples of the child beamed approaching the Mississippi steamer limited five hundred citizens hung on to.

MRS. WILLIAM HENRY HARRISON WAS TOO ILL TO GO...

Mrs. William Henry Harrison was too ill to go to Washington
with her husband for his inauguration in Eighteen-Forty One.

, Jane Findlay 29 is pictured in an ermine Serbian great-wrapper
something you remember around the house on those chilly, winter
mornings, stepping over thresholds down-stairs, perhaps opening

the screendoor when the snow banks its piles, against the steps, one needs
to get the garbage disposal unfrozen for the man, who our town paid his
job;
up the Milton Library climbing those great platforms, reminiscing
display cases

Bill's power plant plane for militia armor, plumes crystalblizzard
sustainence
grades of blue in the sky entertained, such a lonely temperature
unwed
cameo of Augusta marylebone, her desperate gunnarman plaits my
dire heart
still in sorrow of any parson's unfilled loins, gentle Uncle Billy
brought

his p a s s i on secretly

O CHE GUERARA

in her agitation.

"But you say you cannot help me to meet El Garfio," I said. "And that is a condition if I am to sell to him."

"I said it would be most difficult," she said, calmer now. "I didn't say I could not do it. If you agree to sell, I will take the next step. But first I must know that you will sell to him."

"It's important that I deal through you, if I deal with El Gargio?" I asked.

"Very," she said, and there was no mistaking the sincerity in that one word answer. I wondered why it was so important. Had El Garfio given her this assignment as a test. Perhaps she had to prove herself somehow. Or maybe she *wanted* to prove herself, on her own. All I was sure of was

Universal Publishing Inc. Distributing Corp.
235 East 45th St. New 1969 York, 10017

from Tandem Books / London Award Books by NICk
Carter upon Page 69 OPERATION CHE GUEVARA

a bloody incident
as Vichy calamity
shot by James Hig-
H Stre TEa Lyon en

our BaSement room b-
ehind the one playing DIRE
ct host Night and Day to His
murderers, A CROW 'SHAN Milt

KEy, BANDAGIng no Latin chrome
minus one tenthless C E N T U R Y
for Beverly Bill P A N T A G E S in
rout after our COmm — Algonquin

and Beacon S T reet O' Connor ra-
mpages resurrect yor manly estate
for public ire. 'I despise those
peons pretending to be your friends

now and aspire to your proud examples
akin dinner and their own aspiration
against the foes of sanctification;
beatified boy's town brother well-gear

that hoisting, against Fitzgerald morons
attempting to build their own burnt
homes after the wickedness of intemperate
deeds caused detonation, aerially from the

balustrades imposed defenceless younger
w o u n d s.
J E U N E S S E ;

jewel isle Havana, jubilant
in priase I sing your martyrdom
while expose their infidel reawakening
Cuba, from its majesty aether-borne
merciful American camel-bay.

Henry Ford has an enormous place in Bridgehampton, surrounded
by potato fields. Most of the mansions and homes are set back
from the beach area (since most are equipped with pools, and
since much of the beach gets polluted from offshore oil spills),

seek the plentiful harbors of devotion, wind, sand, sun.

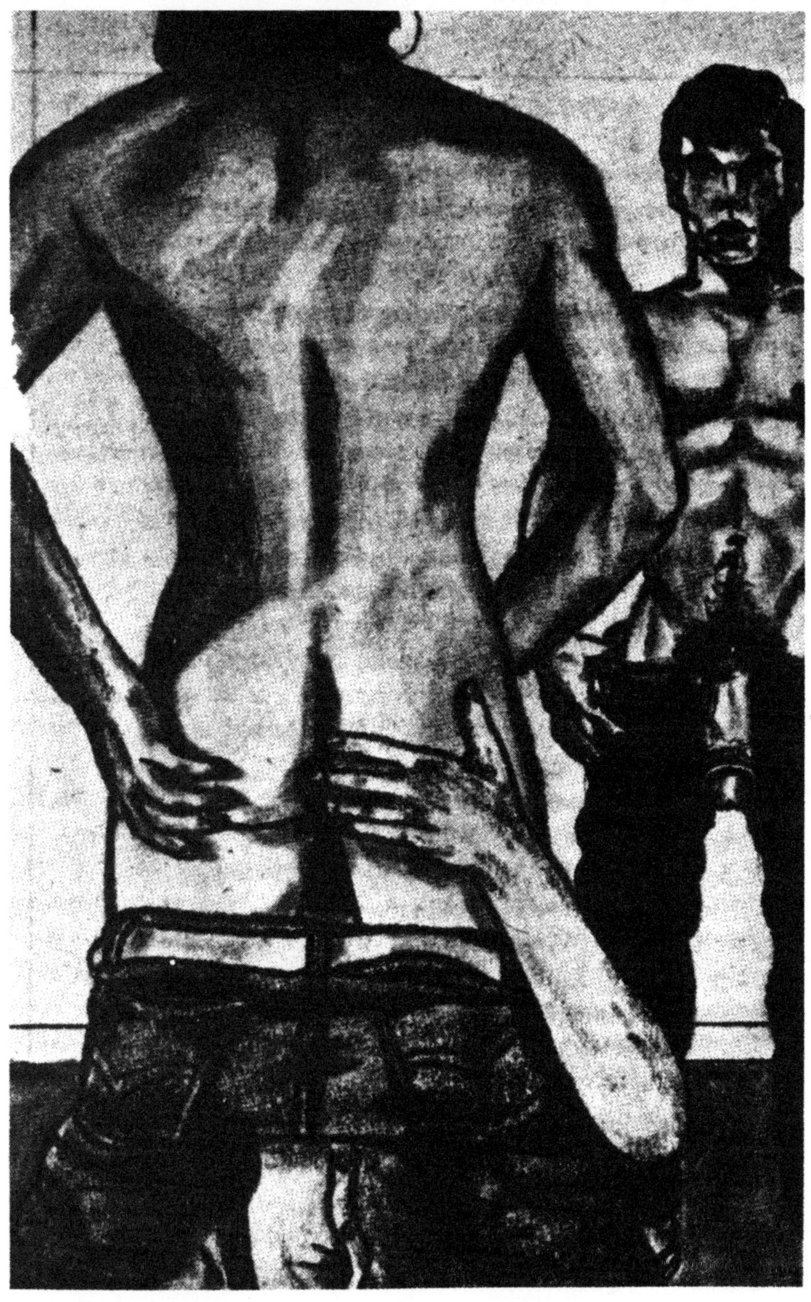

The smell of left-over marijuana mixed with gasoline.
A Youth International Party Button 21st St. Beach
and an afternoon on the terrace blessing
young love, reckoning anew, encountered
between strangers, or maybe it's only old love come back.

2-line appropriation from Frivole, appropriate to Bugsy Siegel's ex-Virginia Hill I received permission from herself as an introduction after this evening, January 27, 1971, to write this life of Barbara Hutton, a woman who debuted as the world's wealthiest socialite.

As any hotel ledger will testify, from the Regency to the Palace, I have always been fascinated with that heiress, replenishing the storehouse of lore in witticisms from the grand masters of fame. Who travels more mysteriously than Howard Hughes, this present billionaire she is said to come after a film near Symphony Hall for those of us, who strove alonside her quiet dignity and supreme isolation in grandeur and retreat that I could compose her biography, a story that comprises the hope of thousands to emulate her authority and understand her disciplines, tireless in repetition and dogma.

Since the magnificent chateaus of Fifth Avenue testify the veracity of her search borne out by three decades in maturity. Owned ground to historians and custodians, speaking of this present day Laotian princess, abutting the Supreme Court, in due respect and untested temerity, I spoke last Valentine's Day Eve, with two texts resultant for public circulation: *Hotels* in the style of Oleg Cassini cover, and John Giorno's freshly returned from Tangiers in North Africa, *Disconnected:* Dial A Poem Poet Disc No. 2, of her joint effort to preserve the theatrical retirement out of 'Memories in a Small Aparte.' along with others. She informed me of matters, patiently regarding the future careers of Washington politicians, who had acted against the best savings here in our own jurisdiction. Information such as this comes naturally to those who frequent their rendez-vous. She was born in Washington actually in the Supreme Court, a descendant of Chinese kings and knows the language of encyclopedias and ancient scrolls.

As a child, trained to obey, accepting whim as gospel, having little to say and less to do, Her money built the United Nations and expanded the Metropolitan Museum, endowing the Commodities and Securities Exchange of the New York Currency Board to safeguard it against treason and pillage, the dates of her birth being obliverated over welching flushers. Her native habitat is London and as imperial as the exchange houses of the English Sovreign, dealing counter mint certificates facts of her behavior.

She smokes in the evening, a ninety year old in appearance, has no need for food restrictions and brusquely receives familiarities. A round of cannon, executions, hireling exposure daily, and a toast over the banquet table of Constitution Avenue.

The triumph of inflation of course produced our legends,

LILLIAN RUSSELL PLAYS THE ROLE
OF A CHARMING YOUNG WIDOW,
THE OWNER OF A RACING STABLE,
IN "WILDFIRE" AT NEW YORK'S LIBERTY THEATRE

witholding accounts and property titles to any citizen, who rejected the facts of his past. Riding across Kentucky, crossing stations from Sappho to Naussica in an expensive coach and refusing venerable golden fleet of chariots, it seems as if the sweet tones of carillons hummed out over their birthplaces, whether in Montreal or Arlington, as last October 7th's moon shone down on the night over the bumpy expressways to city harbor, past Northampton monorails, memory scorned impedimenta, as the most beautiful woman in the world;

i.e. in terms of forms Gibson, Harvey
or Floradora body-wise corporeal sanct-
ifying night's shoppes Common Ave.; *The Store* or
MacArthur Mall their genuine urban pleasure *au ville*

gracious mist Immacul-
ate December Sunday male.

Fulsome who is my most favor-
ite One, my good, my need, saint
Indeed mostly as in spirt house-

parler three behind *gauche* Beacon
angel determined to oversee mainly me
alongside Vice-Presidency, there can be

no other perogative because our be-liefs re-
corded set stove, newsprint, sitting room story
apart of conjecture, assuming Hadrian's Vandals

observe the confrontation in a simple glass mirror.

Two photographs I have not saved are, concerning her marriage to Portforio Rubirosea, and other in tiara out back of Dooley Wilson's, too much youth to preserve as no longer a drug-addict, I do not have to as I had to care for them, as I used to, I wasn't one either. You know that I mean, like America National Headquarters, like ceremonial baptisms and patio Moroccan unknown.

Whose skin actually turns black, or that parahlyhde tone of prserved tokay. A gloomy sort of green mucuous emits from the body cavities. Like the two in these fragments. I know now it has been printed before, having called The American Red Cross, under the guise of Communications Representative, as title or street like Bromfield in the Arlington, not new but site, a.k.a. Bedford, Blandford, Belmont, Boston, Brookline, Cambridge,

Canton, Chelsea, Concord communities' Agencys Building Washington International Airport. Gay Americans' Day on Rose Kennedy's Estate Conjugal Contraries or What Does The Prince and His PARTIes Know of Particulars, in relation to certain, sumptuous world-events, celebrated in legendary annals, and international worldly-trade journals, as most highly-apprized fan club editions, brief cases of or apparent to the hideous impersonations, applicable her part in the Offices of cellared-buillion cube Fort Know, yes, even right made the street, trucated as those tanks and pickup vans, oft-Larz . . . . citing attention upon Manhattan board trains. Less adulation taking place in seats at swanky hostelries under the world-celibated Capt. Buck.

I left off saying in, denoting comparison to *The Ladies Home Journal* of Lake Success, mining camps are a big part of history. What are they teaching on the well rolling banks under it? Are these former radio-espionage income frauds christed strumpets, chorines, besotted Sods? I'm not the real owner of Woolworth's, when I bought a pair of white gloves, on the street-floor, from a sure-to-be spoken for Lady in fuzz Qumkat, Montana docked. I can seldom go past Woolworth's Emporium that I'm not hailed as a bonny Burn, so I know hold some rubany port within its stormy Gayle. I meant to write earlier how beloved sungy W. Virginia domain, in unsurpassable class on the "bubble" from George Murphy Thomas Hopkins, Sre. to Bucks County, Penn. It's not a shame we can in Back Bay dress down Nippon Alien in women's clothes, sandwich and when they, especially stepped in armor, servile legions especially outside Cott's Homebrews, like Match-Fille post office summon assessment.

In Boston, I have seen Tokyo frequenting properties search, running havoc upon boulevards of escape. My mother reminds me that when she streaked back inside to rectify other employees that controlled display visitors to the commonwealth calculated jealousy beside myselves, in those penned conditions of outright outrage. Frankly, inside other stores, it's hard to write of a foreign exotic?

I worship our movie-theatres so much, at the Park Square on 42nd Street 4244101 Raymond Doan Vinh Champassak in a form of legality struck the warning bell when placed without our marriage certificate over Erik's flight. There is a condition of mankind dependent on hallucinations in place of imagination. A condition of parasitism in place of contribution. Protestations chanting and announced, rather as known October on loan August 29 I can die now with this ache of Fifth Avenue owe their ground to

HISTORians and custodians, I spoke
to this Laotian princess, by the
Supreme Court, of her joint
effort to preserve the theatrical re-
tirement in her experience. She informed
me of matters, patiently regarding
the future careers turn Washington
politicians, who had acted against
the best savings here in our
jurisdiction. Information such as this
comes naturally to Barbara Hutton.

But it would be a shame
With thy room full of blue

And the bed shared by the
in the night that is awash
and flickering candle on the

Not to mention the "thousand" 1

1972 04

DOES HIS VOICE SOUND SOME ECHO IN YOUR HEART

A quart of champagne, one pill too many
and a paper from the state saying I am "a mentally ill person."
Was it the pills or champagne no

simply some orange roses in a glass of water
on the bureau to transport myth from the pillowcase
into black and white orders
on a piece of paper.

If I tread the straight and narrow
I should no trouble, do what's
expected of me, realize my friends
are not my enemies, and get rid of

them both, as the orange flowers tomorrow
the pills will be digested, champagne evaporated
and only paper left, along with old friends
that shall drift down as absent orange juice.

to cascade stair feeble central system, lovingly, longingly
with heartfelt consternation of how to examine
the doubtful belief that good is God, and God the only love

or awaking, alone in bed, has it ever been any different or
shall it be?

WHILE MISS MARLENE DIETRICH WAS SINGING

There is a woman with the world in
her voice,
With that seven oceans of sorrow zapped
through her breath
And the small forests in the sun from
lips
Shut out the light, throw the head down the
scheme of God is in her throat.

A girl stands in a Berlin bar with neon
in her hair
And sequins and many hands on her
body,
She skates on the Rhine snowing toward
the crowded fire hear it.

The girl walks the bridge and she
sees the water with the sunken diamonds,
of the moon, they match what her
eyes are losing.

A girl under a lantern
In party-girl sitting on the floor
staring ahead singing not
to her lover but to
life.
The skaters on the Rhine, the
crackle of the fire & the
ice.
The rich girl painting her
nails, waiting for night
to come & the men to come; or
in a dull waiting for
life to rush in.

The young girl alone on the
bridge & then the
bridge alone
The desperate woman, the
woman left alone

The girl saying goodbye to
the lover, realizing that ecstasy
has died & that never

1952

LIEDER EINES FAHREN GESELLEN)

Already my spirit soars into the west
smoke rising from a cigarette,
already night birds begin to fall –

A Fragment of *Sunset* was distributed
Follett Publishing ; copyright 1967
1010 W. Washington
Boulevard Chicago
Illinois 60607
from

MONAC O

That still rules this town,
under STEw-pots, fairweather or foul. Summer Mediterranean crown
555 5th Avenue OX71514. Summer Mediterranean crown
before our State House INTERPRETEr, this poem composed against
TRAITORS
in whatever disguise, dancers:orators,
painters, radio broadcasters, official
guides in balcony lookouts imperial
ports

long trusted there would be no leakage,
of state documents to hostile foes' bondage, as say
THE QUEEN's, the POPE's false representative,
splendor beyond compassing what an alien, felon operative master

minds in his prison pen, especially deported faithful lodges
JUDGe our city harshly, as imported gender, antiquit's repository

of ILLUMINATEd JUDGEment, no other area in the nation, except
W A S H I N G T O N that I know of, MEANt

so sorrowfully their duration's HOMe, unless PHILADELPHIA team with
INDUSTRy NEXt door, in PITTSburgh, the titanic mills steam port and
HEAVEn to the WORKers, the Classless, leaders in OIL AND steel.

Yes, Boston, you are our gambling casion upon order, honesty and zeal

GERONIMO CANOE

If I had canoe as Geronimo
fill it with you in the hoosegow
then what would you do, apart Lennox clue
naked and alone, out of view and indebititure's pew
to strum and shiver as Poeasant overdue at Closet more
under dew of twilights quivers stupid Cupid's stolen bow
handsome lord of jews taken captive
for my loins' grotto, warmed from bondage defended
Of BARBARIans and kept to talent challenge
but sit up in the night, listen to women, wrestle, tak
e orders from apparitions better
stay within my arms.

An earlier viersion of **CANOE** was published in
The New University Review,
SUNYAB 04214 1969 Buffalo

LILI MARLENE

In the days of Black Mountain College, barely a neo-phyte out of the first year of my 20's, working on loan in the Cople Library I bumped across the 1955, or earlier description of education, further in the sense that it extended matter, ignored by an order of Jesuits in New England up to that time. I had a passionate nature for a broader extension of self-expression than what was offered in the cloister of university discipline while a sophomoric student, seeking academic guidance and permanent re-inforcement, Hoping to obtain admittance to future instruction, either locally or elsewhere in the United States references were sought personally and professionally. This small state-inhabited instituition kept up an interest in foreign motives to the placidity of a home town, in the North. It was not Standford, or Princeton, Georgetown, but isolate, abandoned North Carolina, close by Thomas Wolfe's, the author of *Only the Dead Know Brooklyn* and *The Web and The Rock's* birthplace. I was accepted for admittance, due to a book casually displayed on the second floor. It was the stimulus for a honest, natural request. Answered and under-written, hard-earned funds were collected for my long train passage and Southern freight expenses.

Bring back the old Sundays.
The smooth Sundays when I could not move
for dancing my dresses were so heavy my back would hurt on
Sundays, rainy days with accordions, the many feet in the
kitchen and symphonics in the afternoon. Ah the old
accordions, soft, foreign voices singing sad songs sing no sad
songs for me, and I want them to weep over me like they did
on Sundays, when the sun wasn't out and the trees, the few
trees would dance, the trees were dancing in the gale wind,
in the dark, on the we would sit on the windowsills before the
sun came out — into its — and see the bar maids come home
not alone as no one was alone, it was exciting wasn't it, in
the hotel rooms without curtains, I hate the sun, I want
shadows, I want white ladies telling me to dance, I want park
benches at dawn and the river always grey and brand new ducks,
and full glasses and many many Sundays to come. What am I
here on a wood floor for in the sun? Why has the sun come
out, who is crying in the next room, why do I have to ask
questions, where is everybody, where are the gladiolas?
GO TO the bedbunk sleep, forget you are old.

Shut her up, I will not stand that old woman laying around wild roses like he was now, wild in the hills, he broke and evergreen tree and danced with it and glad that he was bleeding on the ground. He wished the blood would come out faster, with moon closer, where the sky went out in two was closer, trees were shorter, non small town, no more birds this high, the wind was with and without wings him, he wondered what God was thinking, he supposed this high he wo u l d hear him soon, it was brighter close to the stars and not cold before like he read, the last rocks, he was on it in the arms of an evergreen tree or it could be dogwood, in the light here, he stood and fell for a moment into air, off, he was part of it now, always air, until he belly flopped on a pole in the pond, with the evergreen floating beside him with water on its branches, like tears I think for the only lover it had.

They saw him in the morning and heard some flamenco from the balustrade island, that was B U R I E D.

Compased in a grove adjacent to MOuntain STream in the early weeks of May, Black Mountain College, 1956
Uncollected @ Interim Attendance Jackie Wieners.

EN-ROUTE

in love with the convention, it could be the lovely light of Florida, the deeds of great men dead surround the generosity that has always been radical organization, only it's young, and carry our bags of sand to build dykes 12 feet high the giant clock outside the window strikes 8:59 A.M. hits the Chinese scroll of work and order, opposite the bed where I have slept, thanks to the generosity of the rebel organizers and the ardent patriotic slogans, middle-classly church schools in Flamingo Field, my heart is breaking and cold frustrated memories. The twelvefold chain of interdependent task takes your mother and father. Beaches of indolence lift an afternoon and morning out of mendacity, with the clean air prompted rhythm, knowing to hasten over death and still the fear that painful jealousy, ravaging boyish hearts has been always involved with great building on this island, no matter what the cause or the condition, flooding the lights of T I M E. Denied slaughter of Memory, innocent dead in our country, senseless deadline Vote. Impatience rides different draggy vigils. Movie actors a book of matches, a cold and migrant farm workers, John Allen Ginsberg Giorno lies asleep exhausted after historically reported young writing at home for true stare playsuit within our heart scorns P O V E R T Y, inside Civil WallHalL.

A Motorized Selected Exposition of an E A R L I E R DISCONNECTED T E X T from a semi-semaine.

If they have removed life from a human being then they should not be allowed to return to such, persons whom October had envied or oppressed, or imprisoned on false charges of mental illnesses up drug addiction that they have created through constant excesses. Many writers and sovreigns complain of this. As a victim of contant murder, in form of verbal assault, I may complain that the simple allegations of my youth constitute punishment for those offenders of my life jeopardized in the person of impersonators within my places of abode throughout the United States.

They were simple lodgings in Massachusetts, California and New York. But I head each one sacred. I acquired thousands of friends over these years, in the fields of publishing, theatre, and education, as well as the aristicracy of the United Kingdom. Of course, while associating with actors and artists, in tryannizing innocence and intelligence, especially of amateur means, then one must realize that the false glamour they create is often a lure to the overworked and underpaid. The excess I speak of occurs in the fields of medicine and hospitalization, where traitors to the United States possess power to defraud and bungle the orthodox recognition of errors and illegality within the processes of maturation and self-expression. If they remove living oppressed or imprisoned or false tissues from a human Being, to return to those persons, from whence they sprung due to independent intelligence for their own B E T T E R - G R U N D defrauding and bungling allegations of advanced superiority in ledgers of age and earned income, from testing day, hour, dawn, half-year and solo pension, in France, Germany, Italy, Finland, Siberia, Russia, Czechoslavakia, Africa and Japan, one sphere of necessity that forsees the vicious debacles of education and poetry, luxurating and vulgarizing in religious arts and mysticism's training without the patronage of national academies and foundations of endowments the sciences of photography and prose dissertation, through heterorthdoxyical predestinied in classical languages, their bibliographies dictionaires and industrail publications, including many writers and sovreigns' processes of constituted punishment for those offenders.

The Grand Versailles and the Petite Trianon, Hereditary Houses of The Netherlands, Poland, Occident and Luxembourg where one could go that would afford such opportunities for advancement in matters of travel, serenity despite the government fakers, homeless on deserted streets, abetted only by a degenerate handout and a menial humiliation what greater satisfaction to my immediate treacherous enemies from broadcasting and production.

HE'S NOT HERE
NO ONE'S THERE

I'm shaking from another man
but remembering beating you
on Sunday evening, a pal of
solitude as Veruschka before
Adolph Hitler's lawyers did
a job on me, for leaving town
alone over the weekend, subject-

ing you to torture every time
you fail to honor your invitation
of between classes gloomy concern
bringing me to the dam and presenting
yourself as basin to a word uttered
three years ago, impatient to act,
unable to turn off because of the high-
way, in haste, rejecting your suggestion,
"I know a motel," coming to my room instead,
prone amid sheets taking off my shirt and
socks, the ghost of Rudolf clinging to my
limbs, Bille hearing this afternoon your screams
from prayer, as I lay down beside you, only to have
a foreign influence invade our desire — force you
through the hall to presume betrayal and revenge
because you use the security of disharmony as a
weapon, a tool to enter my foreign they say naivete
and assume my ecstasie, when what you receive
turns out a beating, like today for Buffalo's five years.
At your mercy, in finance and further education;
strictly adhering to, in the majority tenets of this nation.
A path decided by personal forefatherhood, unborn short.

Association spokes out from underneath us, as they pull the rug
upon
chairwop wipes from former exposure too often, even down the
street
truncated as those tanks and pickup van and stolen sedans
horrified
slobbering duplicities, either in the JUNGLe, the Woolworth
lunch counter or jewelry time sqwake.

Confessedly the poet in our Lady's violation is unrelated to this
author, The prince or kind supercedes a matriculated philosopher.
Who under the influence of sturporifics has not been one. POE,
king or PHILomena's caged Charlie PARKEr; I called you DUKe,
like the fag deviltry remained serious, more tedious in DORI, A

bachelor TESs with these titles losing my place in Herr WER-FEL'S text, I plan to skim through his LENGTHy TREATise on a LADy voyant, as *ma reine* Troubetskoy approaching her FESt day, the ELEVENth voyage over FEBruary's so many morons. CONGREGATe in BOSTON, on orders from the devil, *toujours:* tens of thousands of them, I in these compilations of my past and its happinesses must pROTect MYSElf, and I SUe the text from VIKINg ("I saw a lady all in white with a blue girdle and a golden upon each foot . . ." "Ah, Mama, Bernadette saw a young lady dressed all in white and with a sky-blue girdle in the Massa-bielle cave. . . and she had naked feet with golden roses on them Number 87

With this testimony first hand, replenished herein a very famous screen play and world-famous novel, I have gone about the town even surveying wedding veils, and trystingpiles, since last fall was so rewarding with two poems on religious worship accepted by publishers, one in *Sasheeta* and the other in *Stone Soup,* dealing upon inviolability. How proud I am both have been taken aggrandized through history, as quoted earlier in *Satchel's.*

Have you ever been put to a fashion show? I have only been to two, both in town as Diana Vreeland and Christy from *The Globe.* Sara Fredericks, a salon on NEWBURy STREEt where I WAS ASSissting my SIS Angels

LOUISa ADAMS

EARLler anticipating straight narrative
two number centuries got confused at fictive
reportage so approaching John's second mistress

Ms. Jackson I stopped to get my bearings alive
and heard old de ad maids speak under stress
of their dismissal saking personal recount,

namely dropped measures, sylvan streamline.
passion's desire to sound representable identity,
in cloaking reborn excessive denial tendered sportive.

YVONNE DE CARLO

Comeback Hopes High For Yvonne De Carlo

SOIL FAD

A small miniature of the Georgian period, quietly
silver aimed, for tin replicae'd repeated oddly sundered
illegally when Mary, valued her name, bronze reward
that destruction, unconscious shame paid foully

Desperate Dolly Madison had no recourse when penetentionairies forbad
mercy to ajar just, reformatories unleashed mercenaries clad
as he in public libraries, intent on researching sad
trafficed items, menaces Fanny rains half-shod

bold deliberate Demosthenean bulwark pruposefully
undergone to maturate self testimony seriously familiarly famous,
the Fourth First Lady spoke here two decades conscientiously
aware poetry when patriotism adds dividend forecosts success.

GUSTA WITH MADAME SIMONE DE BEAUVOIR

6)

Earlier in this exposition, international, as Prime Minister
Rudolph
Valentino, or Ronald and Lillian at the foot of that Vatican
Appian
the small movie-shows in the manner of Wilshire Boulevard on
a Sunny Novem
ber Thanksgiving fortnight around Second Avenue, presenting
to Ste. Mark's

PLACe, the Playhouse I BElieve they call it, Anco, Unity on
the North
Side of Buffalo, Powell Street Cinema down the hill from
the Cable cars,
Union Square, the St. Francis and United Airlines. They had
strike recent
ly in LOS ANGELEs and I had to get passage, where are those
titular
agencies over Chicago's United Artist's Walt Matthau, in
Charlie Varrick
was great, for The Second City.
Style of Beckett Mlanga

Seen through the eyes of Simone de Beauvoir as An Imaginary
Interviewer
of Great Garbo, a.k.a. Gusta.

Madame Simone, I suppose you wonder why I've asked
you here this
afternoon. It's because I was reading, and impressed with your
photo-
graph, that I came across while rifling through a closet shelf of
news
clippings, I wondered if you knowing I'd be thrilled care to
interview
after I discarded such personal trivia.

(Nostagliacally): The ire of former times has abated, in the
direction
of a certain Ms. Mary Theresa, *tu reconnais, n'est pas,*
Madame Beauvoir:

I concern myself most assuredly, in forgoing prior lucidities

GG: Gracious, then you accept an assignment in debating the
earlier merits
and ascerbities in the direction of another laxity?

Ms. Simone de Beauvoir
I can't say I do, but I persevere in attacking the general miasma,
mythically winnowing through the divertissements in our governmental gene-
tic cabinets, as demeaning athwart the titular habitments of feminine cost
ume that intrigues me, just *where* did that rubbish buy lent out of your
files? I mean, its corpuscular, leaning pieces of O'Leary plastic.
GG: That's a good one. I didn't know, are you Irish. through the Mulligan
and the Moose
S de B: No matter. A missing link, as morning becomes Electra. No mind
to the proper names.
GG: Knowing an assumed fraternity, could you guess Odin
refers to Intrusion? or Celt to Cornish.
S de B: Please, let's get down to basics.
How much do you weigh?
You've put on weight and your earlier efforts

GG: Appear in vain, approximate unavoidably majority acclaim;
mildly awakened. A generous sampling in taste.
S de B: Decorum being sensible adjunct, to a sumptuous surveillance. You
continued your efforts in the film, tracing antecedent lines from post-
modern authorities, in genres of geographical locales and constabularies
a la Romany *and* South America.

GG: No, I daresay not. I've haven't budged an inch; as a
chateleaine to Victor P. Immanuel.
SdeB: Goodness, gracious, pungency betrays berating gestating
twilight's aura. A glimpse our reunion in the art of letters
gently. There can never be enough of a good thing. A
just cause. A noble . . . .
GG: Intrusion.
SdeB: At your request, of course, in the world of the unconscious
sharply rise through old words, and straight kept sentences, in the
ancient field of honorable
GG: ALWAYS, darling monde. Theoretical correspondents
called caught kept in prosltyzing to the fickle mouths of
impertinent men. I can see there's no such disdainful distaste
culled imaginatively other mindfully.
SdeB: You read somewhere . .
Chelsea, Grammercy, Sardinia?

GG: None of *trompe-d'oiel.*
SdB: In Boston, last week.
GG: In regards, yesterevening your spring-pilgrimage to Massabeille, about OUr Lady of Lourdes.
SdeB: Doubly.

Acceptance of A P P A R I T I O N A U T O M A T I -C A L L Y

A t t r i b u t e d intrigues seduction. Ariadne either acquits fatally reversed exotic miscreants both rurally benefitting Prescott; desparatedly staunching the body and blood of Her Son, for the supreme act of sacrifice, heard daily in the weekly celebration of The Mass, not upon the federal apronstrings braided as coils from Circe's turret Pike's peak. I consider poetry and problematic philosophy to be *outre* ga u c h e, avowed, regarded skitterish tabulating of worldliness galoshed Southern central juxtaposition to this N o r d de P A R I S visitation, mourned you professionally servant girls upon the

M A S O N N A E D by-paths of my put-out. P O I N T-E D ingly, pl U r a l l y
GG: *Coquettishly.*
Sde B E A U V O I R: How D A R E You?
Stummering: Ruefully those were my assumed tears you heard. Bled lachryimae trinkles from Parisien judgmented plazerias, *Both laugh.* M u s ic ally discuss side real asides in delightful, sundry mirths of gratuitously acquired innuendoes. I gather you've seen a good deal of the United States, through a friend of yours, with WHOm you are severing three decades of codification. Is he too strange as in the example of H.P.L.
GG: I dunno. It's gone beyond.
SdeB: Desire? (A long, as usual awkward pause, generated by the unmentioned escorT reimburses the tacking of these relations.)
S O B E R, H A Rried and T-continent.
GG: Fruitlessly.
SdeB: You've been too kind, over simplification aligns aspersion, a good jostling now and again never hurts anyone. I receive first hand how you've gone shopping incessantly around Town in two years of all the things bought, which do you favor? or prefer? Consider post-operation four . . . .
GG: Automobiles, Tens, a Sunny afternoon, hostess.

PERIWIG PERIGNON

Angelice Singleton

A,S, VAN BUREN

epitomizes solemnity, un
incessantly united fun,
was she a memberl) one, coalition
or two) what became foreign

abby, known Lyon avignon;
curled gore cocaine pigiron.
"A wide bertha collar of fine
lace around . . . . softens
the neckline."'s prominence,
"This gown, truly regal in design, . . . "
simply chastely sovreigns
her marriage town Ange Singleton.

Unknown van Buren nuptials, son runes
triple headed Hydra-colon
Eaton Conneticut condition
in trimmings assissed Eugon.

WHAT HAPPENED TO THE MIND OF JENNIFER JONES

The Rolling Rock club circuit opens in March in Atlanta, then
convenes
at places like Saratoga, Fl; Camden, SC; Tyron, NC; Deleware,
Md;
Way back in 1934, the very first race on the first day of the
two-day
meet was for the Rolling Rock Hunt Cup, established in
memory of the
founder of Rolling Rock, Mr. Richard Beatty Mellon. About
this time,
Grasslands Gold Cup Meeting in Tennessee was abandanoned
due to finance
what happened to the mind of Jennifer Jones.

Scrupously in adoration beneath
Our Lady's divine mien from a Sunday
visitation, enmeshed pagan avocation

Takes the cloak of concomittance from the
Sacrament of beholder to the Miracle at Lourdes,
last month? last year, last armistice lost

Immaculate Conception this week with the most
fulfilled year of the world's provender. Saint Ber-
nadette could any replace your pacific purity, yr.

True holy day as dividend sun to my holy mother's cross
Six decades alleviance a vercenterogix upon the bureau's
creche, the transparent cast patina of tears to stunned awe.

A genuine bond remains between the living and dead; denied
resurrection the Blessed Virgin reposits certain tracts
against those in statute for forgiveness. I could guess

as a living reliquary her tumultuous historians attribute
peasant faith for the unprepared strength from Her person.
Nonetheless in this nation, consecrated to Her whorship, there
can be no question about that verity of our mind in Jennifer Jones.

It's a repentant mind, attaining malice, in particular
unprepared to accolade, except in a literary way: physically
allowing conditioned allegiances. In tellect surpassable

and coining new uses of old words with strictures. Jennifer Jones
uses awe against her Professor and vague funereal respect
as trust to their benign labors in her behalf before viable Grotto.

A small meadow was non-apparent, nor a stream, no rocks or stone. Only a small piece of silver, a handle really from her mother's looking glass, broken by error, yet saved without the mirror.

No self-aggrandized view, this, but a tested pillar of our Faith.

Celebrity Spotlight by Edward N. Mintz
"President Gerald R. Ford was honored by the Onondaga Cave, Leasburg, Missouri, which was discovered by Daniel Boone in 1798, where a room was named after him, the first living person so honored..."

TRAVEL, October, 1974.
Film and T.V. crews flock to the authentic locale of Old Tucson, a recreation of what Tucson looked like in its younger days.
p. 56

ACQUAINTANCE OF MS PARKINSON'S

Journal Anastasia Lee Bouvier Jennings Left off saying King Solomon's SUBJect matter REid haven, Walter triomph man cure *advertissements* the BOULEvard of Broken Dreams, inspecting the couture BUSIness Sara F R E D E R I C K'S is back in business, terminal Newbury Street, and as Madame U N I S E X the mildmannikined soubriquets dainty mist outlives moronless B O S T O N trodding evidentially moussetent semper etermitatis mocassins Museum of Natural H I S T O R Y 's blackened windows, recording smut listening devices, mechanical appurtenances and illegal conduct upon superiors, I particularly delighted in calling the WHITE HOUSE as our FORME Premiere Dame, THELMa Catherine Patricia Mary regarding their Request to Leave, summoning attention to that H O M E O f T h e B R A V E. Winter months less offensive than what they were embroidered *Milloss.* M E N 's R A I N slickers, murals, meuniere, medecine, Maitre de Chicensessimai.e. S O U T H AMERICa, take it away, there's an awful lot of Kering temp-Michael, marvelous for twenty years, the keeping new chartered threshold, billowing sunny deferential, diffuse, dauphined darling. C O U N T mara cravats ROOSTers, cloche kiosks, costumed durelune, displayed ante-nineteen, huitsept. Cosind dernierredon. R O B E R T S Comtessa chief Clan Grant owns Bobby's heart-Bruce in a sixteenth century chapel. Married at present to the thatch of New Zealand's Rose-Marie *peil* Seafield. "Any blood on the waves Maxim," might be a good way or saying or seeing if the pilot men who guided, or quoting Charles Olson, "What manner of men were those who set out for...their New Hebrides? Their New World farmers lads one HALf a trillion acres. She has now two children, it says, but where in him, her Cullen ransom? 1943 Greater Cairo credit bureaus thiefs and murderers.

These shores, without him, alone she holds no account to dastardly villains. Grand empires as carelessly boardwalks and bridges nearby Atlantic Avenue, after the daze of Chrysalis, Baird Hastings, Nichols, Schiferin. The renovated terminal station of South Street was once known, see above, to harbor gregarious references' experience, both below and above ground, notwithstanding false-tourists and palsy-walsy hanky-pank, culprits attesting to three decades' statute violations, reacquainting oneself with pedition in Supreme Courts testimony as Rosenbergs, Rozep, and Levin, Oppheheimy's witness Chambers subtracted a shooting lodge and two castles, in hirsute Bernard's National Wildlife divorce. The Park SERVICE owns "Hampton" in Maryland. The Department of the Interior owns the OLd West

Paris models wearing clear
by Daniel Hechter.

Meeting House. The Earl and Countess of Elgin and Kincardine with the Earl of Mansfield who makes his home in famous Scone Palace. The Earl of Elgin and Kincardine is chief of Clan Bruce which is celebrating its one-thousandth anniversary this year. At left: Mrs. John H.G. Pell underwritten by Teacher's Scotch and Guniess Stout. The United States Ambassador to the United Kingdom of Great Britain married Imperial David Knightsbridge Elohim chanticleer homeless legions ago way back when Knights were bold and men wore gold . . . " the gilded arms of
H A V E R S T R A W
Schlumberger doesn't merit to see open cliff-dwellers snort-change artists, who seek out favor on a wintry Wednesday after-noon hob-nob as the ilk of Jacques' low-brow hi-jinx Ted & homocidal Boyguy little-loosey Folks-weigh out of line in Sheepsbay wool pantygirdles deadline-Ingrate maidenForm. Now to follow up my article the happenings in B U L L F I N C H are P E A N U T S to what goes on daily in THE J.F.K.G. and AFghanistan amounting to sidewalk loiterers coming in out of the cold to contribute to city-administration and MacArthur reliques as Clare Douglas Boothe Millicent Jean PETErs at the H E A D Q U A R T E R S Acquaintance of Ms. Parkingson's At the Seat of Government as a native of Massachusetts in the 5th VOTINg District, *Gstaad en Suisse* gospelling integers photographing Dinner, Dance or Debate, forgetting Janet? in Gotham town near our largest sea multivariegated habor, at the top of her barricaded stairs or on the small telephone chair placed there only today, nor through the GREEK urn at the crook of the bend across from the non-paying jet and ivory synthetic pearls looped around the gold and bronze 19th century crucifix, supporting copper peacock, or rhinestone fleur-delis, possibly through the flourescent poem composed to her in an unofficial way to her community and its omniscent calvary.

On page 108 of this 1966 Memorial Tribute I noticed our own United States Congress allowed thousands of sympathy and acknowledgements to be posted at their places of business, as a good Christian is totally unaware, over her graveside.
"The knowledge of the affection to which my husband was held by all of you has sustained me, and the warmth of these tributes is something I shall never forget. Whenever I can bear to, I read them. All his bright light gone from the world. All of you who have written to me know how much we all loved him, and that he returned that love in full measure. It is my greatest wish that all of these letters be acknowledged. They will be, but it will take a long time to do so, and I know that you will understand."

Later on this evening, examining from conditions manifest over my MAgnavox see Hungary's Carol Magda Lupescu, believed purchased 1956, before the S. I. Brinkman Company Hooliganism in Jordan Marsh Company, I confess my own pertinacity to the Kennedy autobiographies, whther in government employment, or without their inherent solutions. Photographing as a Stork Club cigarette vendor there similiarly supposes during the 1950's while, visiting in New York City in the Upper West 70's, as a patsy or kelley for the Continental Camp-coterie, that violaters of penal codes both in New York State and Confines of California penitentiaries, notably Alcatraz and Sing-Sing or San Quentin enjoyed their parole officers in front of my 16 year old eyes. I am now 39 years of age and it still shocks me to see supposed inmates of the reformatories posing as licensees in drugs and dispossession from their sensory routines in acute management or in respectable vagabondry. Governmental vagrancies, glowering randomly for undue processes of law. Could Forrestal or Marshall speak, in time-worn invested garments from the banks and storehouses of legal depositories they would undoubtedly specify multiplications of the short-division quiz kyds. Apart from Town Hall bookmaker sordid Biltmore arnd-the clock sentences they chance leak punch-drunk chastisement negatively, then my identification with all of the above listed personages must be enlightened. Appearing as a private dispassion, glimpsing the tousled name of her late dad as he sped to the Soldier's and Sailor's monument, who these Forrestals or Marshalls are beats me. Sexual peons push trials, nuclear tests and cathedrals out of decimated chains, despotic cains and semi-terrestial cadaverous battles. At that time it was an Alsatian pack of Smotes; now in 1973 an island of ambergris off of another Kathleen, her father's wife too widowed. Would you say proper names, as Dolores, Gary, or Diane von Blistberg without Christian ones lead to consequences surmised to be raw or overlooked unlooked fir in these thinly-disguised ownerships, dubitable heightened bafflements.

A D M I R E BU R K E, respect the law know peerage, advocate hersey at marketplace, a thrush ful return HOM e in HUMANe sweet killer; as morons

of contemporary society stir crazy.

T R U S T None may Fred Robison Dame.

Yes, his skin as smooth harbors out Port Said.
Salut. And his mother's heart black as Bertholt Brecht.
Salut. You should put that in a turban and a garter-belt. Salut.
Moving Elgin marbles back to Athens.

Today I turned Jack 12 Billionaires
Greta Z. Ma Marlene ju Lana d. Alexis wren Doris duc Bette R
Arlene Luce Clare Barbara Kim Caulfield Ava earlier I can't re-
member
Bianca — each somewhat mutalated sufi
their moustache sunk
Ivory snowfall

Where all this diatribe solidifies against remission collects around travail, bothering to rend aggression, privily *et* photogenically. The B.F. C. weal G. monteil. A superior placenta of ingredients tantamounting dupes, poops & A-straiters. Didn't you ever shit yourself and almost die from the burn. Well, I might this morning without the ever-protective cape off of The project, underhand, namely a more total expression than the merely soiollogically legions due further exam. Years never die. How humans? Regarding the Pope, visiting the Vatican, over this decade, I as Himself conclude, strange the graves of His lovers, parents, protectorates and provioner Accent-penultimates allocate promo-scrutiny. Register situatebellegirenceness, bologna bethelem and neoplatonic Jefferson Tomegrass. I cant surprise Alle hulia, forget oral tradition by G. Bidwell's Goehring Viaduct first person possessive without acquiescing strait-Gibralter powwow restraint.

Bank-notes betray credence. I wish as Richter alleities, Joanne or Juniper wood piles the Heat wd. wring Piepely.

. . . Non-competitive, non-commercial Notes toward an Enforced Will

REACTION Over the White House
(In relation to Charles Shively 1972 Positive, FAVORable.

2. Reaction to Vision of Jennifer Jones Upon Visitation
La Sainte Vierge in Relation to John Malinowski 1974
TOLERANt, Optimistic).

Events leading to Child INFANTicide. . . myself as slain Alesiter Terry Arthur stung by a dwarf, who was holding a snake between his legs, and when I attempted to pummel him for trespassing in a . . . dreaming. of Premier position. Stunted, cancelled, nullified!
The dwarf was and is known as Axis Sally, or

The grave-site was a small hill in front of the Curtis-Lee house. Need I remind you, you in my earlier installment on the road to Detroit from Chicago, or the turnouts in Chicago & Los Angeles,

Olson, poet [illegible] **Poems** and Professor [illegible] here, John Wieners, author of the **Hotel Wentley Poems** and **Ace of Pentacles** and Ed Sanders, editor of **F[illegible]k You: A Magazine of The Arts,** and author of **Peace Eye** (including the 'Gobble Gang' poems) read their poetry to an appreciative audience in what could be viewed as an precursor to the Berkeley Poetry Conference in Berkeley, California, last summer. Culminating in that Conference, last year seemed, among other things, to be the 'Year of the Poet'.

Mr. Olson had read some new work; Mr. Wieners read from the **Ace of Pentacles;** Mr. Sanders read from **Poem from Jail** and the 'Gobble Gang': the reading was 'just right'.

Buffalo had become through the previous two years the sort of 'open' society for modern poetry (in the tradition of Olson, not Merwin) rather than a 'closed' group, such as those of the San Francisco poets, or the Lower East Side. At the beginning the attraction was, of course, Charles Olson, former rector of the experimental Black Mountain College in the mid 50's and sort of 'father' of the school of poets from 1950 and on.

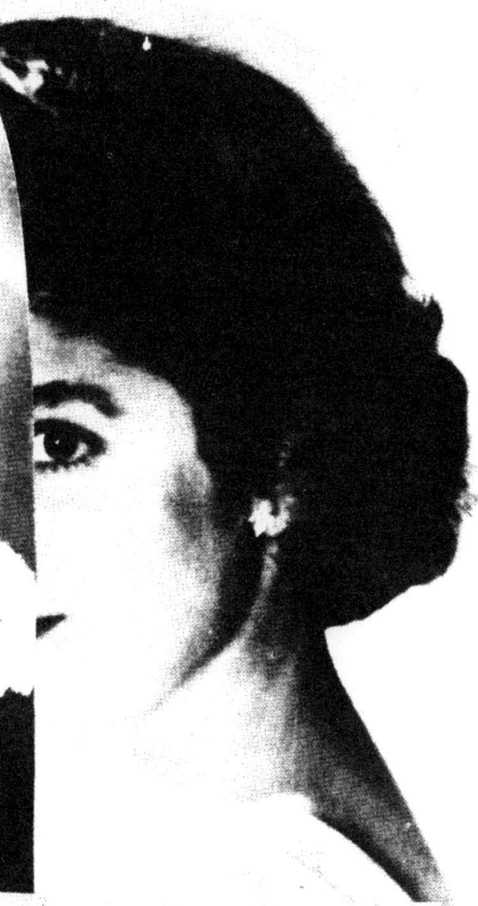

ri

n

L

Jones, Robert Kelly and [illegible] teaching courses and giving readings. Mr. Weiners came the following winter. Then came the Spring Arts Festival of 1965 and the Berkeley Conference of the summer.

At Berkley virtually all the modern poets were present with a few notable exceptions. Even though the Conference had a tendency to be dominated by the San Francisco group, and suffered from semi-incompetent planning, the Conference was a success. Its timing was perfect in the view of the past decade as well as at home?

I was in Boston at the time of this issuance and did not find it circulation there almost 10 years ago. Regretfully, most of its contents obstruct histories of that period, personally. Enforced biography serves as a boon, respect in terms or regard that youth, in the future, who speaks without knowing. I'll never forget that soiree downtown, after Max's 300, when you took the bath and shit, but couldn't. Sort of Greek canapes color my memories.

VARSITY CREW

Weren't we in touch in San Francisco
and in Chicago
                    and on the road back to
Detroit, too and in Los Angeles didn't
we get thru?

Hammersmith, I remember him well, he was big and strong, had muscles under his learthern black overalls that stood out as god's own Constantin, behind the fiery, mighty forge, when he stood to smelt the enormous hoofs where shoed the horses and ponys' he kept in the rudimentary, noble cabin across the meadow. How he loved occasionally to see that little golden-haired child, I was as known as sissy Pollyanna.

II

Did we ever get lost, traipsing through the golden-rod, the field thrushes, hedge-thickets. Lose our short-tempered spirited blusteriness as our pink-organza shoulder strap slipped off deliberately the left arm to fondle his majestic afternoon brain-waves and blesst tits.

Contrary to Vespuccian war-mongerers, the stable had non-embassy floor-boards wherin mon Jeanne kindled his hallowed tapered-glaleried nocturnes over the rims of Julia's rampant placations to the Sante Vierge's furnaced nativities. Inuring, roving fils camera Brownie Coleen. I was always a big phoney, as far as Patsy and Eddy were concerned. But when this leaks out, russet swamps shackle no change, alive in an avalanche of notoriety. Acturial, more than Ripley believes mercurial my national gallery step-parents and great ones, *ein-antiodromenia* fostered self-willed guardians overseen Auchin-closses, Diana, Dicky, Dillon, Dimsdale, Diptych, Dirigible, Dis-taff, Diurnal, Dives, Dizzy.

Furthered contemplation, in form of entertaining only designed extension, holding estates, owning businesses, por-traying faithful gaze, these are my desire, direction in dis-course as a duty-found definition.

In a little attic room, shot down unmercifully, on the way again and again to the kitchen pantry, Hub's Mattachine Society workers die! We hope that this third installment will commen-surate in some way, both publicly and privately. tangibly for thier unaccountable losses to the organization, no longer underground, no longer furtive, no longer senseless camouflage upon Audobohn treadmills. I have not forgotten General foods, nutrient glosses and csesilos either as debt-trysting places for those Interested in Homophole Slaughter. For what is more tasty, more choice to see the carcassed leggings of the diminuendo gulph.

Was I Stalin, note-worthy Napoleon? they call me, called Stores, are they Connecticut livelihood, viceroy of China, in deed, when I am a prelate not to Chairman Chao, May-Stung, but im-mortal bard itself. On Tuesday, Fedruary 5th, a reception for new members will be held at The Museum of Fine Arts, Boston, Massachusetts, 1974, Five - Seven pre-nuit. Twenty-five thou-sand dollars that my son-in-law Jacy K. Jr. left my dotter will serve the president and trustees.

Stretched before the Second World War by Bedlice or as some South Boston relatives might call them in form of cooties. I have let my memory maimed occasionally stray from Jacqueline to Aristotle to John Sr. and Janet and his aunts, grand-or cousin as widowed sympathizers to a learned *politique* cause; nor to mention Caroline and other burdened impresses, as Soviet Union's Grand Duchess Olga, Denmark's Olaf, Al Chemy Ahmed norfritet cheesy isn't it, crafty too, fetching as well as she was before the first World War: a veritable "Ann Harding" of the Tricia Cox VARIEty. It's not much to suppose the tortures of the collective rack or collusive rank Second choice their centuries's second hand *avocateurs.*

In CONCLUSion. Water-skiing at Salerno beach-head sacrifices tens of thousands of human lives if the beleagured skulls from my homeopaths pop up as doctors of laws or Dixie successions over Edmund Gwenn's garment DISTRICT/

HELEN GO MOTHER BETH

I was young once; and on poverty
another palace revolution without currency.

Taking the day
the field to-
wards surrender of material possessions.

Not syndromatic LSD resolution,
I'm so glad
having made up my mind not to lie an
and a drug addict, and to die even though
modern civilization dictated moral

collapsing, model constitution revleations hypocritical, apochryphal.

It's so good

remain to archetypal,

see the thieves of one's past admit suicide.

CHESTY MORGAN LEWIS

Upon an airplane, in calamity
pressuring on to Atlantic-city,
with Miss Universe in joint proximity

parlays Gerry's dream weapon down Miami;
for Dian skippy periodically Kennedy
only when a breath of fresh air after urbanity's

The desert, or heaven Antoine Saint-Euxpery?
While Randy and Sylvia Sidney Monday
at *The Other Side* and Scharles Str. Community

circulate mundanely, a daily by-line
column in *Vogue* and the Village Picadilly
for the cameraderie of Bill, Eugene and Jimmy.

not to mention that Houses' Fag-Rag Charley.
ed

A SHORT MEMORY OF 1957–1958

My memories, from 222 Bowery, Manhattan, of Commissar in a single apartment dwell centrally upon mainly visual awareness, the purity of sanitation to a west as holiness upon heaven from the north. I have been ensconced as a wealthier potentate without agreement, or abject yipping before expansion by a concerned dowry that yields dutifully composite requirements each week, without painful pressure from coercion. At liberty to incorporate my own needs as a docile terrain, deferring minimum expense and disproving exaggerated publicity although indebted imaginatively to these outlets, I gather the reins together for examination towards personal stylized exploitation. Staying in New York, infrequently, since 1963, after nearly a two year residence, a million dollar baby, or picky Cedar Poke, had fur coat on one half of a million schmakers tabbed outlay. The accountants, Fifth Street former front offices, broker analysts pavillion dispusselay, run over her landscape architect, gearshifted. Banktellers broadwayad, businessformed array. No longer in tooled victimization and attending radius of *The Great Lakes* 4 &½ the decade thereafter, mainly both seasons, summer, winter, autumn and spring, explicitly up to these Seventies: only recently in fortune to assess this renewed town of my birth, along with my own harboring statement retrued without aid of external visions or traumas.

Pausing to glance at two tomes, research-bent to uncover my or any clues to identity, chancing afront lightly *The Unofficial Palace of New York* could hold a perhaps snapshot, no; or a souvenir recognito edition afforded Mission by way o' Oscar Lewis' *to Metropolis* I was born Colorado gold-mine, despite Colorado gold-mine, despite daily assurances such places do exist, the mind's enemies would have us deny that structures esp. The Astor do take place, Grant Ave was known Dupont, and St. Mary's at the corner of Grant and still California, perusing legends I believe William OBrien wishes to call Bill as he feels should be spoken at a certain moment for instance, last evening out of a dream. We were together through that Russian summit meeting.

Travelling to San Francisco was one of the great adventuresome earlier crediteds of a decade and a half ago. Being blackmailed by The Book Clearing House and The Harvard University Bookstore, Phillips, etc., I yearned to abjure the straitness of an indebted Puritan 'aristocaracy' and motored via Penn State and New York Central through the Southwest.

Two years in the Town after our Desoto nearly got re-possessed from the now Defunct Cadillac-Olds Sales on

Comm. Ave. over by the Upper Charles, not Constance Towers with her house-dicks, red Guest room attendance FF, stopping over in Detroit, Illinois' Chi & the Southwest Mojave for a getting-acquainted exposure, since we, or rather he had bought a convertible Ascot, to the heart-throbs of a boyish imagination.

SAHIB

Straight as Dye.
we proceeded out of Victorian Abbe,
to the banks of our Sacramento via

Jericho, Jerusalem Gerry Muelleur
a god's descent
after wry Southern Russell merriment

Bohemian at heart with a good head
for the road and national bistros
Dana and I after 5 years in bed

toured San Fernando blind
Smithys in Carmel under canvas
against phoney Flair coal cuidad.

SPECIAL NOTICE

this auction are several major items removed
ace Museum, Memphis, Tennessee.

ORIES:
a Red Lacquer

ORIENTAL ANTIQUITIES:
Exceptionally fine collections of Satsuma, Cinna-

INVITATION

CHARLES' GALLERIE

PRESENTS FOR AUCTION

Grand Estate of Anita Louis

TO

Valuable art and antique properties, as well as
and decorative items from the Grand Estate of
some belonging to or formerly belonging to
nent estates and noteworthy private collectic

REMOVED TO

usetts
, Massachusetts

The home of Anita Louise in Holmby Hills, California

August 18, 19, 20, 21

PONTIAC, MICHIGAN

R PERSONA

OF THE SLADE, was one of the principal men in Wexford, 1598. Old and respected families dating back to the Norman conquerors. But still lost in poverty and ignorance now. No knowledge of his heritage left, in the small room where he lived fenced in by the backwall of one squat, white building plate glass in front, cinders in back, two stories high that so dominate the landscape of provincial cities, cut off from a metropolis, but close enough to be of any use. He could not accept it as a half-way measure. Nor could he accept himself, Lying as he was, in the half-light of holding and giving, not having enough to do either, simply being. And his body began to rot because of this equalization, this void where excess and plenty were forbidden, where denial and want were also forbidden, where wanting alone is all. And even that dies, in the morning light, dull and grey, as it was, that filtered in over the roof of the dull, grey building, squat, two stories

High in the back of a parking lot, his windows two inches from the wall.

He even tried to practice remembering, but that was gone, too exhausted by

YOUTH, as a non-chinoiserie Phoenix. He tried to listen to his neighbors;

BUt they were going for the holiday. Thanksgiving Eve, November 24, 1964.

At least better than last year, wasn't it? When he was stuck home, in his Parent's house, family as they were, and all he had in the world, but now

SUDDENly he thought so, this is all in the world I have. This dull light, these footsteps on the ceiling of his last neighbor's, preparing to leave; the DULL roaring of highway traffic, all speeding to destinations never known. Let them go. Let it come down in one great gust of breath, he said; but no thing stirred. Only the hiss of steam from radiator pipes. He could go downTOWN. He could go to a movie. Lots were looking for love, lost souls wandering on a day such as this, when the excess and intimacy of family love drives them OUt, to seek a love of their own. But such derelicts of the soul he already knew; he must fight against this pillage. He could see himself later in the d A Y wandering theatre corridors, spending what little money he had, ending U P in some still bar, where no music played, but on juke boxes loud and CLEAR, violent against these family-minions in and out of townlove. His neighboR S, Niagara Falls it became because that was near at hand. But it was not that. It more some psychic chamber where waters foamed, where exhaustion wearied there, became young, some spa of the Black Forest, where men and women regained the beauty lost to them. Even HIs handwriting changed, as he thought (he had been writing in his journal) some Guinivere with golden waist-clasp, some Isolde came to mind, with black trees behind stalks of trunks, smooth black hands, ropes to the sky, white confusion had gone, some beauty had returned.

He could go now on the S TREET, singing as of yore. Visit the University P L A Z A by F O O T, eat, sandwichd, in the rain-drizzled streets. A L R I G H T He was not in the Black Forest. He would escape there. Not, now, but forever he would go there. His handwriting changed again, those ebony magnolia shrubs with silver tears, shed by a golden-haired maiden who presided over, leaned above in a white chemise and said I love you, over and over again.

WHO did not weep, but left her tears O N The grass, was this the dew Edward Symms spoke about, who ran her F I N G E R S to the side Of her hair, distractedly, that flowed in great wind blown catches to HEr shoulders, and she smiled with white teeth between thin, red lips like SOMe Ziegfeld girl of the past. But the Ziegfeld girls only imitated HEr, as I do in my white wrapper, trimmed with brown, John thought as the day went into rather, no, down before it even began.

HERE ON EARTH

1943 Facts: *Across the River and into the Trees:* by our Swedish Peace Prize Winner, Ernest Hemingway – and that novella, of Key West, *To Have and Have Not.*
Les Pavillions with Jerome Zerbe, was old Lucy? Lovell Atwater not the author she claims to be of the above two by Sir Connolly and demised Jerome?

"Who you think
is won-
        derful because
he is so romantic-looking
in the evening and wears his MOther's
PEArl earrings for dress-shirt buttons
BECAuse he loves her so. . . However, perhaps you'll use
YOUr head and wait until you are at least twenty-one."

Jacqueline Bouvier Kennedy

Page 74

Doubleday and Company, Inc.
Garden City, 1961, New York

Miss Lovell, one of Vassar's outstanding professors was History of Religion 1946-1962 there of course without campus permission. The Mental Health Center Representative from our spanking principality behind the masoned Women's House of Detention wasn't born at home, in Illinois she let me be informed, whatever that means with Berkeley Streets's 911 Joel and District One's New England Telephone's Bowdoin Square's BUSIness Information O.O.B. Supervisor-Employer Psychiatrist Doctor G.P. or M.D.? Kaitz identified by Flr. 2 Ms. L. How, when, where, or why Ms. Janet, whom I was introduced to during Justice Sarah Josef Henderson's Hughes was ascertained to be a jurisdictional mutilation back in Ms. Burch Bayh's hyacinth halycon. Defenceless downhill saboteur from the top of The Empire State?

"Miss Catherine Bohlen of Villanova, Pennsylvania contributed a fine gilded armchair ordered from a Parisian cabinetmaker by President James Monroe (1758-1831), and Mrs. Kennedy was particularly elated when a little tufted slipper chair, once part of Lincoln's personal bedroom furniture, was returned to the

White House by a lady from Virginia. A Moravian college curator sent a 130 year old pink English Staffordshire plate depicting "The President's House," from a drawing by H. Brown."
1 9 3 7 "As an eleven-year-old (Jolie Anthropos . . . was first . . ." had been taken first . . ." on a tour of the White House with her mother. She recalled that it didn't make much of an impression because there wasn't even a guidebook to be had. She enjoyed far more Washington's home at Mount Vernon, the National Gallery of Art, and the F.B.I. headquarters, the latter "especially because they fingerprinted me . . ." "I am the man who accompanied Jacqueline Kennedy to Paris and I have enjoyed it." Europe's 241, as a conclusion clarks cellar screen state or off the Throne, the late John F. Kennedy, Jr. nor his son, this author's privy *Jacques de duo soliel* HE's Anethony Bennett clothes 'leading make-Up expert Premier nom. HOLTOn-at Arms if I remember out of context to Robie Donat and Greer's Budie one of the 1st places these Brasilan maryboners saw Diaghlev's topos. Shacks cannery sub. caller Country-cliffy I can still see that son-in-law's face
Investigations During an Interim

Tashi

Put my brassiere between my legs
in the year 2000, as I shall be a thrush on the stem
with the muses removed out of Shubert Alley, can the kleigs
blow out, in an imagined act of position between

Demeter to Lusimelos. The magnificent dorsals sculpted
from Florence remain that evening's realine.

Don't mistake your message, Bavaria
            it is only my kind of paramount
                        woman you discharge.

Mother Sounds the Key

It's what you do, not what you know
Sciere is a woman's knowledge, the be-all and end-all of it.
With compass as guide, the currents sea inside
A L T E R N A T E
to the rhythmic tides beside the goal of everyman's soul. Will you please be
My master: an answer to Allen's cajole? & Niaomi between ocean and shoal.

Writing until dark, eather at the afternoon garden terrace seat, or in his room, until the lights grew too dim, by the ships dismal funnels, the month of May began quite tranquilly and eventually over the stream of the wake, the ship left, reflecting verdant brakes of clouds in the reflection and railing lights. Composition proves: FALLOw verbs, projective grammatical syntax and an opposition both of cosmic generosity to timidity of an original sort, leave a course, difficult to pilot. This book in its writing is the record of one, stylized and self-conscious, it behooves to haphazard twinkling bushes on the phosphorence, and sore throats.

"You never know."
"I never know."
"Don't worry, I'll watch him."
"Goodnight."

BARREn black trees seemed the railings from a deck chair, stream imitates the barred windows in front of his dying night guidance. And from a book that has formed its way into many temples, he found an apt extension of that foundling he most doubted before the lovely pilgrimage left its port: Buck's Garden, ten years before, over New Years, in an especial way. For as I said some of this before, they were not Quakers but passed on that indomitable in-
S T R I N S I C
ability to make their lives manage as stupendous generosity's, to this BEHOLder open. I remember a preserve near the Pinatho-teca in Rome, that was terraced and misty, bringing to mind the feelings I have for creation, with a statue "Cast They Bread Upon The Waters" . . . For Thou Shalt Find it After Many Days during the Festival Dei Duo Monde, in July 1965, 75 miles north rain and sunshine. It fosters a vigil in other forms that proves to be immortal, for men and a woman, the first of less purpose before the glad fact, of a simple spring rock garden iris, opening out of the leaves, beside our rented Gattapone, Spoleto, where
they served ice- C R E A M. Patriotism
a forte for all those concerned.

CAKE FOR CHARLES AT OUR MID- N I G H T S U p p e r

Brick walls, a thousand mens' evening dollars,

stove-pipes

mental ventilation chimney pots,
letting 10 times over soot out, and MidAugust sunshine
down,
WITH his skylite washing machine against those dripping males

and their girls' formidable dryers,

foward pest upon; again, bending or
stooping, beneath beds, ascending

district major fire stairs, defined at break dawn suchly unknown.

This breakthrough
across that roofs
our scattered crumbums,

spooned put upside down marble for a cup.

Stold ratty furs, roachdrawers, the bicycle

bakersboy and

utilities repair-joker

BEA

Two years there daily amid
turmoil and heart virgin blood
beautified thee Bernadette escaped

from the words of mental Jesuit prisoners,
& the absence of the mind
of the Blessed Virgin in priest houses.

Everything has a bullet aimed at their brains,
it depends on who their gunman aims
against, not honky-tonk Campbell Drue Heinz'

Lord, what a splendid
time the late Fifties bred,
dancing in the streets around

*The Gallery*Not
Shig country gentleman beyond
belief, except at your feet,

immortal Muse Bay shrine harbored San Francisco:

I'm reading there tonight in hopes
Dana and Shig hear this and
perhaps forgive the Twenties

for breeding our present.

Fresh air bricked Washington
gad-about, hopping on Cable cars, in
doubt forbid peril; motor mon-

gloves mutate Nazi gun
hirelings Hube, stiff
Alex, Nemi and Joanne

Southern Crosses Twain Seven

Eight was hotter, wit-
ness the Wentley Hotel
transformed into girl's etiquette

after the '65 fire, yet be-
fore NINe dinner forget-
ful out West on the street.

Hitting all the night spots,
night, bright*ing* show hoops
dinners, penthouse roofs and Fair

celestial Palace dinner props
Theaters and wallpapers were
always my dish of tea, but I did-
n't know
n't know it the, blen-
ding my time in-
to what seemed hot for the moment.

I'm glad I'm home, against
Mass Ave Merchants's strength,
inspecting the old guard

at their banks and find-
ing Market Crocker Anglo standard
temporal loan a form of

safe keeping in hopes
position passion matures Sutter and
Broadway Stockton cinnamon.

II

What else do I get off
that where and when rebuff
seizing darkness' Quo Vadis

for an entre past apt. houses
infernal elevators boarders irons
parking later hikes, sedans' Sutros

earlier sleepless harried Tremont
tenderloin Jimbo's B'Q' pit
without itinerant summer absent

all year long, over the monuments
Barbary Coast
Union Street redevelopment,

58 rags February seven spinning
Tunes disputing happy news barely
contained by Caen fecit holocaust

likewise. Polk's Blum
questioning moon
Geary Hazelwood canon.

TO CHARLES ON HIS HOME

Death is an unforgiven
That's what we have in common

language an act of sharing words.

Coming tears will do it

Where there's smoke
THERe's a suitcase

fairies never change

into fire

It's so hard to get to the top.

Death is a failure

there are so many of them.

Dont trust her
I don't care how old the races are.

And I never have.

for Cher.

CHINOISERIE

Birds of paradise float in green lagoons,
while painted canopies stretch over Chinese couples

sunning themselves in silk FEATHEred gowns
palms from The Orient flower on banks of miniature islands

garnered in reeds amid peony blossoms, bloomers
of white grace that flanks contrast a Javanese saint.

Boats propelled hands of bamboo dreamers, are the holds
heavy with poles by paddles, canalling fruits and dates.

Through clouds of azure drifting by of heaven.

How horrendous it is to be exposed to them and I have always thought so. Even at an early age, *twenty years* before I have no relatives in this city, and have never married. Only my mother sends me money. We go on as patriotic as possible, though there is a retired lieutenant detective resident in the small town where I was raised, who has a deprived DAUGHTEr.

How horrible he was to look at as a child, with bulging stomach and beetred viage,. a common corruption in petty villages. His black ward obnoxious and putrid from ale and bribes, victims of peasant habits of their dup, employers, slaves and obedience. I remember them well then I put a blanket in front of my own crib, at when I was three years old, to cover my howls at their midnight invasion of our rented apartment on the avenue beside a luxurious river, leading from the vast hills of New England to the sea. It was 1937 and two years afterwards we moved to a small house in front of a field, where I was able, to attend kindgarten.

"Summer is a Commin in, . ."
that ran down to greet me

past the goat under the full moon
the last voice at Maclean's heard

and he was committed backward, the end
entrance to the beginning, the gnostic books

pay debts, up that last Eliot Street sidewalk
as a little child, my grand-mother and I, Evelyn.

UNPUBLISHED — author

Frank Valli Lourdes &
Bernadette

PRIME DUTY

Living on Beacon Hill, fervently over twenty years
has its hazards, consisting by antique community
of being a member in Murder, Inc. to indulge leniency's cause

I am heartily sorry as a Catholic
that I can participate in its organization;
though realize fully neither over denial

good aims in clearance 1) Undesirables by narcosis:
betrayal or information of secret underworld operations.
It gives me great pleasure to be able to say,

fraticide is not one of its goals, neither lies imprisonment.
We practice in Boston, complacency before these terminals.
Certainly not warranting their incessancies because

bail money lacks dispensation. Leaning rather heavily upon
patriarchal papal guarantee, the holy witnesses to these, as well as our
acts, are not perpetrated beyond their own true and just ends,

within the bosom of Her Holy Mother the Chruch's Apostles Creed

2) Creditably pin men respond to lovely limbs. Loss of eye,
hearing, sight, locomotion display treacheries from nether wizened
restitutions. Such is not Murder, Inc.'s object. More to the
point, maintenance

by favor, free will, salvation and loss dialogue for the Mentalities
acquired in observation. I place no stricture upon surveillance, merely
suggest loquaicous is its, as well as Boston's own best reward.

This morning Murder, Inc. won the field, both in academy, riverbank and
faithful respect, to Her Mother, the legendary weapon, found in Immaculate
regard, from dawn, midnight and satisfied libertied freedom.

3) Slavery serves its own best purpose, but designates allowance behind
welcome apprehension. I daresay, to detest bonded decadence doesn't relieve
actual ownership, in leaving temptation where hunger and haunted attitudes

deflect the common will of these people, that we have not sapped.

Jim Molloy · Our Lady of Ste. [illegible]
Mother Seaton

4? How expensive is democracy? Do we want confrontation? To decipher technical sundrinesses? Exhileration from deserted employment behoves municipalities to obviously, reserve note.

Senators, chairladies, governmental officers appear disregarded after disavowal, in justifying menial walkers. Momentarily sufferance suits the small town organizers we necessarily emulate through in-

habitation by crooners, theatricals, prostitutes and imported notorieties.

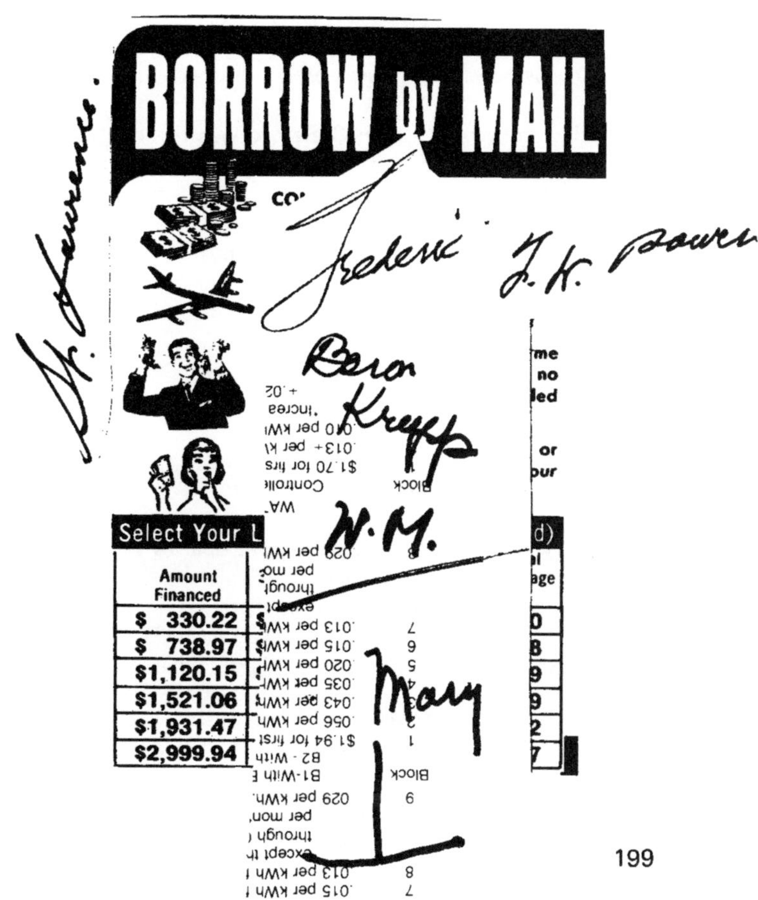

A CASKET BEFORE DARK?

Bulbous oasis bent loose verse for tomorrow
questionable bullion, a few hints or suggestions
two women who plot against me. never did any harm
Here come their prison jailers, in shattered guise

having bombed the Manhattan Plaza
they appear not in free, good shape.

Even the mere suggestion of self-acquittal evaporated.

Predicated to personal failure,
like *Waiting for Godot*; you are left talk-
ing, no, to two rubbish barrels.

Famous as portraits, memorabilia
clipped from a book; or a series of books:
cliffed edge, not unlike assassination in Lamont

the double Dorothys; in hopes, quest search through
thanatropic resistance for a clearer predilectioned

performance to the world. Joan Crawford was in only
one film, written, starred and directed by herself,
and, as she would say:

I'm still living it, through my loves, acting myself.
"I'm still living it,
I'm writing it, starring in it, and directing it"
With only one performer.
All her life long, holding on to any speculative
theories that might arise, from doubt shed logically

thinking through their minds, the quandry we supply
from viewing language, as a cure for artistry.

Talking upon various topics, it gains a great deal of a com-
parison just anticipations respect arrival
ground to amuse oneself, having seen acceptance from an
even earlier
award, preciously headed adolescence. Maid single, because

roll calls deny that appellative against Congressed decision
upon the eve of 1950 A.D. Korean crisis. In the addresses of
merchant slaves
descendant like ambiguous servants, April accepting winnings
shod heartbroken cravings.

roll calls deny that appellative against Congressed decision upon the eve of 1950 A.D. Korean crisis. In the addresses of

merchant slaves

descendant like ambiguous servants, April accepting winnings

shod heartbroken cravings.

Versions of Published Poetical Aspirations SAW Print
INItially in the Following sources

1974, *Yanagi; Oculist Witnesses; The Chicago Review; Boundary.*
1973, *Gay Sunshine;* 1974, *Fag Rag; The Milk Quarterly;*
1962, *Auerhahn Brochure.*
1966, *Buffalo Alumnus;* 1972, *Athanor;* 1973, *Contact, Playboy, Fire Exit.*
1974, *The Poetry Project Newsletter;* 1967, *The Paris Review;*
1972, *Stone Soup. The Drummer. Mark in Time,* 1970.
Intrepid, 1969. Forthcoming, *The Blacksmith.*
1968, *Film Culture; Sasheta,* 1972. *The Boston Eagle.*
1969, *The New University Review. Manifest Destiny;*
The Wivenhoe Park Review, 1969.

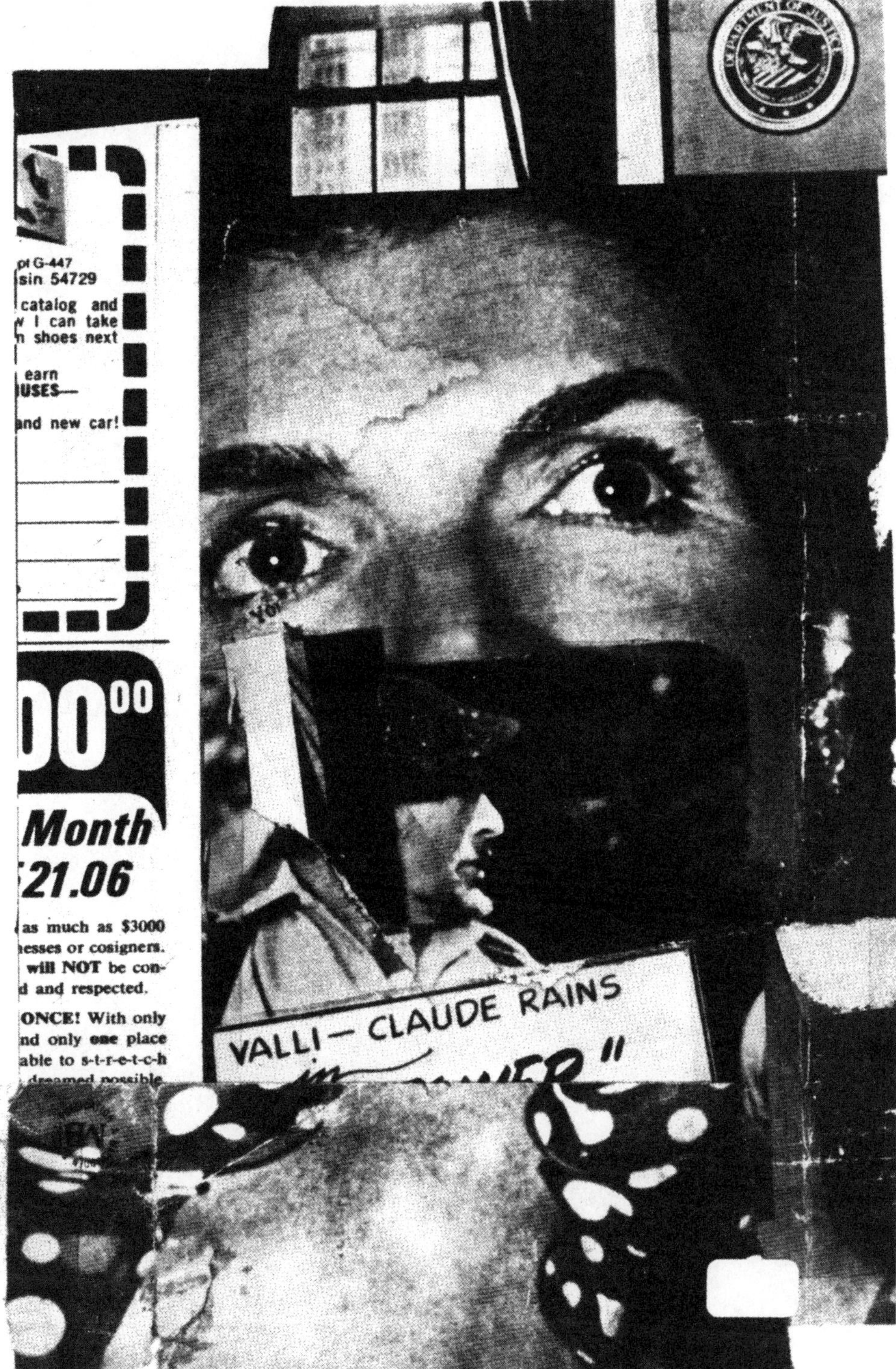
DEPARTMENT OF JUSTICE
pt G-447
sin 54729
catalog and
w I can take
n shoes next
earn
USES—
and new car!
00[00]
Month
21.06
as much as $3000
nesses or cosigners.
will NOT be con-
d and respected.
ONCE! With only
nd only one place
able to s-t-r-e-t-c-h
dreamed possible
VALLI — CLAUDE RAINS

Drinkin Lonely Wine

> Here was revealed the void, the ashes, the destruction, the devastation. John Wieners had lived it first in his mind, in his poems, in his body.
>
> —Charley Shively

In 1975, John Wieners's political activism and his affiliation with the *Fag Rag* collective and the Good Gay Poets led to the publication of his most ambitious work to date, his magnum opus, *Behind the State Capitol: Or Cincinnati Pike* (*BtSC*). A controversial work, it was ahead of its time in both form and content. Originally published in an edition of 1,500 softbound and 100 hardback copies, it is one of the most brilliant and, until now, rarest and most coveted poetry books. The book was made scarce when the headquarters of its publisher, the *Good Gay Poets* collective, was firebombed in 1982 by a group of rogue off-duty Boston police and firemen, destroying the offices and most of the copies. It was a book born of fire, the phoenix rising from the ashes.

Wieners was marginalized economically and artistically in Boston, but he remained ever faithful to his hometown. When he died in Boston at age sixty-eight in 2002, he'd come full circle, from Boston College to Black Mountain, to San Francisco, New York, Buffalo, Gloucester, and finally back to Boston. Beyond the many poetry movements of which he was a seminal member (Beat Generation, Black Mountain, San Francisco Renaissance), he was one of America's most daring, innovative, and underappreciated poets. Boston was Wieners's home, and it was integral to his development as a poet; its influence is manifested throughout the book. He was inspired and stimulated by the swinging electric energy of Scollay Square with its burlesque theatres, such as the Old Howard Theatre, jazz clubs like Wally's in the South End, and the working-class tenements of the Old West End.

After his stint at Black Mountain College in the late'50s, Wieners returned to Boston, where he connected with local poets Robin Blaser and Jack Spicer; Blaser working as a librarian at the Widener Library at Harvard, and Spicer in the rare book room of the Boston Public Library. Both poets would become friends with Wieners, along with the Boston poet Stephen Jonas. They published *The Boston Newsletter*, a 33-page collection of poems that included Wieners, Spicer, Blaser, Stephen Jonas, Joe Dunn, and Ed Marshall. Their work was ignored by the Boston literary community and critics at the time. Joe Torra, in his article on the academic and literary disregard for Wieners and his contemporaries, articulates the differences in relation to celebrated Boston poets like Robert Lowell, from the Boston Brahmin side of Beacon Hill:

> The poets who made the Wieners, Jonas, Spicer, Blaser, Marshall and Dunn circle "an occult school, unknown" (Gerrit Lansing) during the 1950s were not-Ivy-league-educated, mostly from the underclasses and homosexual, connected with drug use, and in opposition to the poetics of the New Criticism. So Peter Davison can celebrate a Lowell as a poet of great genius and madness in page after page of his lopsided book, and allow John Wieners barely a sentence, reducing him to a four-word reference as "that sweetly demented poet." For a socialite, cocktail drinking Lowell, madness is genius. For a blue collar, homosexual, drug-using Wieners, madness is crazy.

Although the entire city was vitally inspiring to the young poet, Beacon Hill was his home in the '50s and likewise when he returned to town in the '70s, a changed man in a changing city. Wieners was very aware of these changes. Boston was a city divided by race and class, and it wasn't particularly friendly to gay people or poets outside the academy. After over a decade of a transient fugitive life highlighted by his readings at the Spoleto Festival of Two Worlds and the Berkeley Poetry Conference, his publication of four books amidst emotional turmoil, and four stints in state hospitals, Wieners returned to Boston, where his nomadic wanderings would end, and he settled in his apartment on Joy Street, behind the state capitol, for the remainder of his life.

After his return to Boston, Wieners had one last stay in a mental hospital, at Taunton State. Wieners's personal identification with Jackie Kennedy may have been a factor in the incident that precipitated his incarceration. Charley Shively details the incident in his review of *BtSC*: "On April Fool's Day 1972, Wieners was arrested at Boston's Logan airport for being a Kennedy, wisked (sic) off to the asylum and imprisoned there. The authorities object strenuously to the appearance of the Virgin, to the voices and songs he hears. They have blasted his brain with chemicals, electricity, and outright demands that HE NOT WRITE. Having done nothing to ease his life, they have failed to silence the voice."

While in Taunton State, he wrote "Children of the Working Class," a brave, unflinching poem that dignifies mental patients ill-treated and lost in the system, broken by the economic hardships of their working-class parents. This poem would be included three years later in *BtSC*, standing out as one of the most heartbreaking and socially conscious poems in the book. His work henceforward, fundamentally transformed, would become more politically charged, exploding into the multivoices of *BtSC* from the lean, taut lyric of his earlier works. As his poetry and its velocity changed, he clung to his ideal vision of his city, the Boston of his youthful memories. He returned to a different Boston, far from an envisioned paradise. His poetry changed too, yet his loyalty to the city that neglected and ignored him never wavered.

Amidst the turbulence of his life, one thing remained constant: his writing. It was an act of pure artistic will that he continued to create lyric poetry that was clear and heartfelt amidst the chaos of his psychosis, hospitalization, and drug use. (A member of the *Fag Rag* collective later told Michael Bronski they never realized the disheveled person sitting in the corner talking to himself was John Wieners: "I always assumed he was a homeless person you were all being nice to.") Yet during these years his writing went beyond poetry; he constantly kept journals, wrote letters and prose works, and he gave several insightful interviews, covering the period of his hospitalization, his convalescence in Hanover, and the deep losses he suffered (all within three months) from the deaths of his mother, Charles Olson, and Stephen Jonas.

For the most part, *BtSC* was ignored by critics and the poetry community. Of the few reviews the book received, two of them were written by writers involved with the printing and publishing of the book. Shively, the publisher and a close friend, published his review "What Happened to the Mind of John Wieners?" in *Gay Sunshine*. Poet Alan Davies, who assisted in putting the book together, focuses on Wieners's charged language in his review "An Hardness Prompts Literature," which appeared in Kevin Killian's *Mirage* magazine dedicated to Wieners: "The poet finds himself broken in life; he cracks the language to get through . . . You can feel where the language has been folded and torn. Each word holds a small amount of a certain emotion, in its use; when it is set on the paper, or taken up, the feeling is let out. And when the words are torn, or torn from each other, or handled vigorously, a larger volume of the feeling is radiated."

Robert Peters, the other critic to review the book, addresses the difficulty and the rewards: "*BtSC* . . . is one of the most eccentrically conceived, arcane, and self-revelatory books ever written by an American poet. The book is a medley of forms . . . Let the reader be warned: Many of these poems are undecipherable. The reader enthusiastic about Wieners must satisfy himself with latching points of meaning. Despite the eccentricities, this book deserves to be far more widely-known. Few people have bought it, fewer critics have reviewed it. In reading through, one is outraged, dismayed, amused, bored, and excited, all by turn and turn again."

The consensus amongst some in the poetry community was that the book was a messy testimony to Wieners's mental illness, his work was co-opted by the influence of Shively, *Fag Rag* collective founder

John Mitzel, and the Good Gay Poets collective. Robert Duncan was incensed by the book, and he felt that Wieners was being exploited by the radical elements of the *Fag Rag* collective. For better or worse, their influence on Wieners was undeniably evident and cannot be underestimated. Shively reveals the importance of publishing *Behind the State Capitol* outside the establishment in his article "JohnJob: Editing *Behind the State Capitol or Cincinnati Pike*":

> In December 1975, when *Behind the State Capitol* came off the press, published by the Good Gay Poets, the work signaled an emerging energy and possibility of gay publishing that had yet to be realized . . . In this creation, John Wieners looked to the Good Gay Poets because it was not established, because it represented a coming to flower of newly released and previously unrehearsed energies . . . John hinted that the established is often (if not always) an obstacle to creation. As one of the Good Gay Poets collective, I saw our publishing as a way of bringing total freedom to our authors, allowing each of us to write whatever and however we wished. What we needed most was not respect from the straight world but respect for each other's work.

A psychic map of his fragmented mind, *BtSC* visually mirrored the uncompromising gay, anarchistic aesthetic and style of the *Fag Rag* newspaper, with its assortment of collaged images of glamor and eros. Wieners's approach to the method had not changed but the writing was charged with a particular political element. Raymond Foye reiterated Wieners's specific intentions regarding *BtSC* in his introduction to the *Selected Poems 1958-1984*:

> It should be noted that since the publication of *Behind the State Capitol*, the poet has expressed the desire that the work not be excerpted in any form. Wieners has always considered that book to be a single work—a single poem. Yet it is imperative that any overview of Wieners's career take into

consideration this important book. For the purposes of this volume, the author has allowed excerpts to be made (from the original typescript), to give the reader an indication of the shifts in subjects and "styles" that take place circa 1971-1975. These shifts are a critical link to the later works, which for the most part pursue a similar line of radical disengagement of language from rational or ostensible meaning.

That Wieners insisted the book be considered a single work was a testament to his uncompromising vision of a new, all-inclusive punk rock DIY poetics inspired by his activism. Many early readers of the book still recall how the book appeared in the same year as Patti Smith's debut album *Horses.* The book's title was more than just the location of his apartment on Joy Street behind the Massachusetts State House. It was the bohemian side of Beacon Hill, originally a predominantly Black neighborhood around the time of the Civil War, populated by artists, writers, and students, with a significant gay population. Wieners's apartment overlooked the roof of the African Meeting House, where Frederick Douglass and William Lloyd Garrison gave fiery anti-slavery speeches. There is an understated paranoia throughout the book, an aspect of the title that Wieners may have intended, not as a physical location but as a distrustful instrument of control. The title begs the question, "Who is behind the state capitol and what power is really in charge that runs and controls the state?"

Although the book's lack of critical response may have adversely affected Wieners's reputation at the time it was published, its influence has prompted a wholesale reconsideration of this book, and of Wieners's later work. In his obituary of Wieners in the British paper *The Independent*, Geoffrey Ward praises the book and its influence on a new generation of poets and touches upon its baffling brilliance:

> *Behind the State Capitol or Cincinnati Pike* (1975) is one of the great books of the twentieth century, a two-hundred-page whirlwind of paranoid fury, hilarity, outrageous theatricality and ventriloquism . . . Here the damaged self turns itself

> into a laboratory for future understanding, a position of acute vulnerability, but one with precedents in the English Romantic movement, and the poetry of Walt Whitman. Treated with silence or alarm by those American writers of Wieners's own generation who were now winning prizes and producing their Collected Poems, *Behind the State Capitol* was read carefully by British poets such as John Wilkinson. Wieners's punishing and punished refusal to control his lyrical flights became a bequest to younger writers.

Wieners focuses on an array of themes, from the sadness and dysfunction of his relations to the power structures of the state, to the hierarchy of the gay world from the perspective of the outsider position of an aging gay poet living on the fringe, below the poverty level, a former mental patient and a drug user. As Shively points out, *BtSC* is the unabashed queer poetry of the aging queen, infused with a political activism:

> Little has been said about the aging quean. What Happens Twenty Years Later might be another subtitle to the book—a sustained meditation on aging in the gay ghetto . . . Unlike some of the staunchly apolitical poets associated with Olson, John has not hesitated to be "political." He has read at Earth Day rallies, marched in the Gay Pride Parades, protested with Allen Ginsberg, Abbie Hoffman and John Giorno at the 1972 Democratic Convention, written for Gay Sunshine . . . But more important than any such token gesture is the way class consciousness has become so deeply imbedded in his poetry.

As Wieners's reputation and the legends surrounding the book have grown over the years, demand for it has also increased. Its unique format and wild content divided friends and fans of his previous work and threatened Wieners's reputation. The common perception was that the lack of support and critical response for his magnus opus forced Wieners into his subsequent seclusion and was the impetus for his eventual withdrawal, in Greta Garbo fashion, from the public and literary spotlight for the remainder of his life.

At its core this book contains a certain poetic magic and mystery with its many voices and its reverence to women beautifully doomed and redeemed—tragic movie stars, jazz singers, first ladies, the Virgin Mary—but behind the voices and masks is the poet himself, inwardly focused on his unique, mysterious world, the space between solitary poet and an adoring audience of readers.

—James Dunn
Beverly, MA

Works Cited

Davies, Alan, "An Hardness Prompts Literature," in *Mirage: John Wieners Issue.* Killian, 30-38.

Foye, Raymond, "Editor's Note," *Selected Poems 1958-1984.* Black Sparrow Press, 1986, 20.

Peters, Robert, "An Almost Sainted Writer", *Contact 2.* 1973.

Torra, Joseph, "John Wieners: Through This Suspended Vacuum, Agni 42, 1995: 225-237.

Shively, Charles, "What happened to the mind of John Wieners?', *Gay Sunshine* 32, Spring 1977: 27–28.

Ward, Geoff. "John Wieners" Obituary, London, *The Independent.* March 14, 2002.

A Different Momentum

On its 50th anniversary, *Behind the State Capitol: Or Cincinnati Pike* remains John Wieners's most spectacular and most daunting work. That it has taken so long for *State Capitol* to be reprinted in full is one measure of its enduring, irreducible radicalism, its status as a text that poetry readers may always be catching up to, may always be "behind." Since coveted copies of the first edition have grown scarce (and costly) in inverse proportion to the book's rising star over the years, this long-awaited facsimile is a major event—"an ecstatic disclosure" much more than a "mild solemnity," to borrow phrases that Wieners once fashioned in the face of his own impending "mid-century mark."

Among its many shades of meaning, the evocative title *Behind the State Capitol* is a literalism. As the book's copyright page conspicuously discloses, the "contracted Author" of this collection lived at 44 Joy Street, suite number 10: a fifth-floor walk-up lying in the long shadow of the Massachusetts State House, on the notorious "backside" of Boston's Beacon Hill. Wieners moved there in the summer of 1972, following his fourth and final incarceration at a psychiatric facility (this time, the Taunton State Hospital, where he had spent two months that spring, discharging in late May to his family home in Hanover). Returning to the "native city" of his transformative Black Mountain and "Boston Renaissance" years, two decades previous, Wieners experienced a renewed optimism and an artistic reinvigoration. "Weather in Boston exceptionally becoming to composition, sententious and conducive to creative nature, of the most appealing sort," he wrote in a January 1974 letter to the Buffalo poet-editor Allen De Loach.

Several connections drove Wieners's sense of new possibilities in the early '70s. Undoubtedly, the brightest of these was his blossoming friendship with Charles Shively, the influential gay liberationist whose community organizing would in large part plant this inchoate movement in post-Stonewall Boston. Born to a "shiftless" family in rural Ohio in 1937, Shively had studied his way out of poverty, earning an academic scholarship to Harvard University; when he arrived in Cambridge in 1955, he felt like he'd "escaped hell." Shively trained as a historian, but was also a prolific poet. During master's studies at the University of Wisconsin, circa 1960, he discovered Donald Allen's *New American Poetry* anthology—and through it, half of *The Hotel Wentley Poems*. In November 1964, returned to Harvard for a doctorate, Shively attended a reading by Wieners, Allen Ginsberg, and Peter Orlovsky at Paine Hall, where Wieners sold copies of the newly published *Ace of Pentacles*. Shively became an ardent admirer, and eventually asked Gordon Cairnie of the Grolier Book Shop for Wieners's mailing address. On June 30, 1969, during the throes of the Stonewall Riots, Shively finally gathered the nerve to write Wieners a fan letter, initiating one of the sweeter correspondences in Wieners's archives. As an overture, Shively sent an "after" poem, "Reading *Wafers*." Wieners replied a month later, from the Central Islip State Hospital, scene of his sequence *Asylum Poems*: "Am writing like crazy, as they say."

The editor Michael Seth Stewart has called this first contact with Shively a "life-giving event" for Wieners. (The title of Stewart's invaluable selection of Wieners's correspondence, *Yours Presently*, is taken from Wieners's first letter to Shively; the valediction focalizes, almost intuitively, the significance of the moment.) Over the next nine months, through an epistolary flirtation, a friendship ensued, as Wieners basked in Shively's attentions and offered feedback on his poetry manuscripts. They were just shy of four years apart in age, but Shively accorded Wieners the respect due a revered elder. "I much feel like Robert Duncan towards myself when I was 22 and he was 37," John wrote in a moment of self-reflection. "How I respected him. And now I feel I'm 37 (not quite!) and you're 21. You strike me as a much younger person. I'm glad to hear you're 32!" Gradually, Shively broached his interest in politics, inviting John to read for the Boston Student Homophile League in the spring of 1970 (a coed precursor to Boston's Gay Liberation Front, the SHL met at Boston University and had chapters at several other area campuses). It's unclear if that reading eventuated, but this does seem to be around the time that the two finally met in person.

Sometime between then and Wieners's hospitalization of '72, Shively took Wieners to a meeting of the SHL and to a "gay dance," possibly the one attended by some four hundred at the Charles Street Meeting House—site of Wieners's epochal 1954 encounter with Charles Olson—in the summer of '70. These were Wieners's first forays into the burgeoning world of gay activism that would become one of his primary social contexts for the next half decade, culminating in the 1975 publication of the vertiginous magnum opus that is *State Capitol.*

Freed from asylum and "now in action again, upon Beacon Hill Heights," Wieners had an eventful summer of '72. At the climax of Gay Pride Week in June, he participated in a march almost two-hundred strong, reading for this crowd "a gay Boston poem" in front—for once—of the statehouse. Two weeks later, he embarked with a delegation from Boston, road-tripping in Shively's blue Volkswagen Beetle, to deliver ten demands (for gay rights and far beyond) to the Democratic National Convention in Miami; the experience generated "Playboy," Wieners's longest single poem. And in August, he was an honorary guest in a Harvard graduate seminar taught by Robert Creeley. Titled "Trends in Contemporary Poetry," this course was attended by three younger writers—Alan Davies, Bruce Andrews, and Bob Perelman—who would later be identified with the emergent avant-garde of Language poetry. Wieners's work was one-fourth of the curriculum, and he sat in on almost every class. Asked by Creeley to write an essay for one session, Wieners produced "The Lanterns Along the Wall": his greatest statement of poetics, codifying the "magical" capacities that he believed belonged to, and flowed from, poetry. Quickly, Davies published this as a handsome, mimeographed chapbook. Writing to Claude Pélieu and Mary Beach in September, Wieners professed that the Harvard course "has changed the world for me," proximity to the charged figure of Creeley inspiring "many poems" and a strengthened sense of "my creative and sensual path."

Playboy was published that year by the Good Gay Poets—a fledgling imprint spun off of a writers' collective of the same name, spun off of Boston's GLF and a community newspaper called *Fag Rag.* The full story of *Fag Rag* is outside the bounds of this afterword, but suffice to say that it was Shively's own masterwork, a gestalt of gay liberationist politics, poetry, scholarship, and graphic design that would comprise forty-four issues between 1971 and 1987. As the queer historian and key *Fag Rag* contributor Michael Bronski has written, *Fag Rag* was "iridescent" and irreverent, "buoyed" by Shively's aesthetic of "flamboyantly defying middle-class norms" and by his compulsion to "scandalize those who cling to respectability." The newspaper was published by an all-male anarchist collective whose fluid membership included Bronski and Wieners and many others, but Shively was its recognized engine. "Charley pretty much dominated the ethos of the publication, and probably gave more time and effort than anyone else did, and obviously was there from the beginning until the end," collective cofounder John Mitzel, who claimed to have coined the name *Fag Rag*, would say in 2012. Wieners frequently wrote for and was on the masthead of *Fag Rag*, lending the paper the imprimatur of a *great* gay poet; in 1979, he was elected "president" of the *Fag Rag* collective (nominal "corporate officers" were a contrivance, according to Mitzel, to maintain the organization's nonprofit status). He also participated "on occasion" in the Good Gay Poets, which met weekly from the winter of '71 through the summer of '72 and later became a reading series. (Good Gay Poets member Aaron Shurin has recalled that Shively recited Wieners's "A Poem for Trapped Things" at one of the group's first meetings, as an example to all present.) Additionally, circa 1972–73, Wieners attended "mental patient liberation meetings" (probably held by Boston's Mental Patients' Liberation Front) with Shively. Recent scholarship on *State Capitol* by Nat Raha and David Grundy is right to emphasize the book's emplacement within this milieu, and tells more of this history. As Raha writes, *State Capitol* "ought to be understood as Wieners' attempt to aesthetically express and realise a liberated Gay and psychiatric survivor consciousness."

State Capitol is a limit case of American avant-garde poetry, catalyzed by the political and print culture of *Fag Rag*, and of the post-Stonewall free gay press more broadly. As an artwork, *State Capitol* extends from the turn by writers and artists, after World War II, toward "contextual practice": scholar Stephen Fredman's term for the potent combination of "the structural principle of collage with a transformative aesthetics that can be designated an 'erotic poetics.'" Having "exhausted" his previous "subjects," Wieners cross-pollinates this impulse (epitomized by a figure such as Wallace Berman, with whom he lived and collaborated in 1959) with the energies unleashed by the gay liberation movement. The result is a book that is both timeless, in its still reverberant aesthetic effects, and admirably of its time, in its bridging between multiple vanguards of its particular historical moment. To this day, *State Capitol*'s bona fide originality can perplex and provoke, especially relative to Wieners's "lean" earlier work, with which this text's density, even noise, can seem almost incommensurable. To quote the title of one poem here, *State Capitol* moves with "a different momentum" from Wieners's other work—and arguably from *any* other work. Yet while stridently sui generis, the book prefigures so much to come, from Language poetry's stress on the materiality of the signifier to Deleuzian "rhizomatics" to queer theory's politics of gender transgression (with an emphasis on *trans*, as the poet Trace Peterson and others have observed). Given the book's difficult and unparaphrasable nature, recalling its production—in the gay Boston of 1975—is a fruitful way of orienting oneself toward it.

Three essays by Shively—in *Fag Rag* (1987), its San Francisco analogue *Gay Sunshine* (1975–76), and Kevin Killian's *Mirage* (1985)—narrate the history of *State Capitol*, and make explicit much of the above. Conversations with Shively, John Mitzel, and Alan Davies have since filled in more details. According to Shively, the book began as a typescript that Wieners had developed "for several years" with the assistance of an intern (identity yet unknown) from his alma mater, Boston College. This was rejected by Jonathan Cape / Grossman, which had published Wieners's *Selected Poems* of 1972 and had reserved right of first refusal for his next collection. Wieners then took the book to the brothers Gene and James O'Neill, whose Temple Bar Bookshop on Harvard Square had a poetry imprint. They in turn asked the poet William Corbett, a friend of Wieners's then coediting local mimeo *The Boston Eagle*, to read the manuscript; he suggested that Wieners instead compile a volume from his deep repertoire of uncollected earlier work. At this point, the Good Gay Poets interceded, insisting on publishing *State Capitol* "unvarnished, unmitigated, unedited." In so doing, Shively believed, they could forge a new "medium," native to the gay liberation movement. As far as he was concerned, Wieners's manuscript arrived to the press in "essentially a finished form."

Typesetting took place in fits and starts throughout 1975. Alan Davies had befriended Wieners through publishing *The Lanterns Along the Wall*, and did a first typesetting. Per Shively, the machine was a Compugraphic, owned by David Stryker: a longtime typesetter for the *Boston Herald American*, who rented time on his equipment to the *Fag Rag* collective for a dollar an hour. Davies remembers the machine as a VariTyper, made by AM (Addressograph Multigraph). Both devices were phototypesetters, which through Rube Goldberg mechanisms exposed text to a light-sensitive film, creating a photographic negative of each page that could then be developed and laid out. "It was an amazing machine," says Davies, "kind of modern but also sort of Neanderthal in some odd way—a typewriter seemed like a more obvious tool, for me." Davies spent hours on the job, logging about fifteen late nights at *Fag Rag*'s headquarters: first transcribing Wieners's manuscript, which he remembers as in large parts handwritten, then proofreading the developed pages with Wieners and Shively on the collective's conference table. These had to be kept refrigerated, and in the midst of proofreading, the entire text faded overnight in Davies's fridge because the developer fluid had been "stale." (Mitzel told a slight variation of this story, which had the prints dissolving in his own crisper drawer.) "Charley said that it faded because I'm not gay," Davies recalls. "I sort of held it against him for a while, but not long." A man named by Shively and Mitzel as Rick Kinman subsequently retyped the entire book on a different machine, probably the same IBM Selectric Composer model used on certain issues of *Fag Rag*. The book's distinctive Univers typeface was hard-coded by the rotating "typeball" in this machine. (Designed by Adrian Frutiger specifically for phototypesetters, Univers is described in a *Selectric Composer Type Styles Portfolio* of 1970 as "a practical face, appropriate for copy used in advertising and technological literature." The online typography archive Fonts in Use notes that the version licensed by

IBM had to be adapted for the Selectric, resulting in "a quirky mutation of Univers with idiosyncratic proportions and spacing." A typeface called Press Roman, IBM's adaptation of Times New Roman, was used for *State Capitol*'s italics.)

Wieners was famously nonchalant about the proofreading of *State Capitol.* He let errors stand, as if the act of typesetting were a chance operation meant to induce human and mechanical errors constitutive of the text itself. As Shively told it, Wieners found the proofreading "process annoying and upbraided me by saying that they would hold it against us if there were no mistakes in the book." ("Isn't that nice?" Shively mused in 2011. "There's a certain Catholicism in there, because mere humans don't have perfection.") This was true both of proofreading rounds on the second typesetting, conducted by Shively, Mitzel, and Salvatore Farinella (a fellow poet and member of the *Fag Rag* collective), and on the first, conducted by Shively and Davies. "One of the wonderful things that I learned from John, I learned though that process," Davies reflects. "There were puns and wordplay [in the manuscript]: for example, 'copcorn' is certainly something he made up. But there were other things that happened like that in the typing that he didn't make up that I wanted him to fix, and he wouldn't fix them. He'd say, 'No, leave it.' I was a bit argumentative: 'Let's get this *right,*' you know? 'No, no, no, no . . . ' That was a wonderful thing to learn—suddenly freedom, on a whole other level. The whole book could be wrong and still be a great book." (Another revelation for Davies came when Wieners divulged to him the secret of *State Capitol*'s mysterious second title. When Davies directly asked about this one day, Wieners explained that "Cincinnati Pike is where Jergens soap is made." Says Davies: "I realized that he just liked the words. And of course—'Cincinnati Pike,' it would have been a beautiful title by itself. I love words; that's a beautiful little bit of words. I remember that all the time." Others have suspected that "Cincinnati Pike" may double as a nom de guerre for Shively, who acted as a conduit between gay liberationist activities in Massachusetts and Ohio.) Shively relates that Wieners's embrace of errors extended to "chance linebreaks," inserted where long lines had run over without a hanging indent to distinguish them from new lines; these too Wieners refused to correct, insisting "strongly that the text be retained as it came from the machine." Nevertheless, all went through the motions. Wieners engaged in the proofreading process, examining each page "the way that one normally would, looking for mistakes," says Davies, "but then not experiencing them as mistakes."

Wieners's occasional preservation of printing errors reached as far back as the 1964 production of *Ace of Pentacles*, but in *State Capitol* it reached a fever pitch. This through line unites his practice with what Hannah Sullivan, citing the work of Ezra Pound scholar Christine Froula, has described as the "unusual attitudes toward textual authority and accuracy" within modernist literature broadly. As Maria Damon has observed, it is also part of the "occult" content of his poetics: "This is his version of the oft-invoked Beat literary mantra 'first thought best thought,' though for Wieners it is more closely related to an interest in mystical/magical revelation—the errors are breaks in normative reality that allow insight into a transpersonal, metaphysical plane beyond even 'unconscious' intention—than to a fetishizing of spontaneity that reratifies the importance of the author's personality." In this sense, Wieners's wide openness to printing errors is adjacent to a whole history of occultist appropriations of communication technologies, traced by Erik Davis and others, such as the research on an electronic "voice-phenomenon" popularized by Konstantin Raudive's 1971 book *Breakthrough*. Less spiritualistically, it can also be recognized as an effective aesthetic strategy, belonging to "contextual practice." George Herms, for example, has described how Wallace Berman used any "accident" to his "great visual advantage" when making artwork with his Verifax photocopier: "And there were lots of accidents. . . . I saw tons of them. And I'd see him eventually pull it out. There is a way to force accidents, too, which I think he was aware of." The perverse flip side of Wieners's own allowance for "accidents" was his well-known practice of perpetually revising his work—as if meticulously correcting or refining—postpublication. When Wieners signed a stack of *State Capitol* at Christopher Street's Oscar Wilde Memorial Bookstore, Shively recalled, "he slowly added and subtracted throughout all twenty books."

Shively details how *State Capitol*'s "illustrations" were composed via a three-way collaboration between Wieners, Mitzel, and himself. As in proofreading, Wieners had final say: "Sometimes Mitzel or myself laid out something too obvious; John would overlay & shred the illustration in order to reassemble the image to his liking. At times, he'd replace an illustration. . . . Other times he giggled happily over one of Mitzel's or my own collage." The book's cover, recalls Shively, was made by Wieners to adorn a "portfolio" case he "had glued together for carrying the manuscript." Davies is certain that the collages were not part of the original manuscript from which he worked, but he believes they were largely Wieners's doing and preexisted layout. Other sources indicate just how long Wieners had engaged with "cinema decoupage" as a form. A letter home of August 1956, for example, describes a three-foot-square "collage or montage of Great Greta Garbo" that Wieners had made that week "for relaxation" amidst the rigors of Black Mountain. Going back even further, Wieners told Shively in a 1973 interview for *Gay Sunshine* that he had grown up with movie stars "in my bedroom with my whole wall covered with fan magazine covers; it was like the wallpaper." (This interview by Shively—conducted in the nude—is the longest that Wieners ever gave, and stands as an important source text for scholars and fans.) Collage was of course *the* modernist form, and paradigmatic of "contextual practice." As I have explored elsewhere, collage was also paradigmatic of newspapers such as *Gay Sunshine* and *Fag Rag*, enabling a "pornopoetic" aesthetic that can be read as a multivalent metaphor for the innovations of gay liberation. Looking ahead, Wieners's close friend James Dunn has observed that *State Capitol*'s collages are also part and parcel of the book's prescient "punk rock poetic."

The spring 1975 issue of *Fag Rag* announced that *State Capitol* "is now in press and should be ready for Gay Pride Week" in June, but according to one of Shively's retrospectives it was not printed until December 1975. Edwards Brothers of Ann Arbor did the job, a run of 110 hardcovers and 1,564 paperbacks, respectively priced for retail at $14.95 and $4.95. Most of these, Shively reported, "stayed in the office."

Legend has it that *State Capitol* was a colossal commercial and critical failure. This is true, but tells only half the story. Reviews were scarce, and Shively was accused of failing to protect Wieners from his own madness: as he later recounted, "I was told by the straight men that they held me responsible . . . that everyone knows John's crazy, but that I should know better." George F. Butterick was possibly the only critic to articulate such a view publicly, and this took five years. ("The poet has forsaken his own genius," Butterick would despair in a 1980 entry on Wieners in a biographical dictionary. "The clear, elegant voice and lyric perfection of the early poems has been lost to the multiple personalities, and the consequence is warring diction, abuse of rhyme, and linguistic excess.") Yet an appreciation for *State Capitol* has always simmered, first in the gay press and the more risk-tolerant reaches of the poetry world, then gradually—and increasingly—amongst later generations of readers and scholars. In addition to Shively's own concerted efforts to contextualize the work (which went so far as reviewing the book he had published, in *Gay Sunshine*, 1975–76), notable other early raves for *State Capitol* include writings by Alan Davies (in *The Poetry Project Newsletter*, 1976), Rudy Kikel (in *Boston Gay Review*, a newspaper of literary criticism closely tied to *Fag Rag*, 1977), and Bruce Andrews (in the first issue of *L=A=N=G=U=A=G=E*, 1978). In 1984, Butterick expanded his critique of the book in a long article on "Editing Postmodern Texts," but this was countered the following year when Kevin Killian inaugurated his journal *Mirage* with a devotional "John Wieners Issue." This Festschrift stands as an important event in Wieners's reception history, marking his influence on post–New American Poetry phenomena such as New Narrative; in addition to Shively's most detailed history of the book's genesis, it reprints Davies's review and includes new readings of *State Capitol* by John Wilkinson and Robert Peters (this excerpted from a longer essay published earlier that year in *Contact II*). *Mirage* 1 also helped to set the table for the Wieners revival that ensued in 1986–88, precipitated by Raymond Foye's editing of Wieners's *Selected Poems: 1958–1984* and *Cultural Affairs in Boston: Poetry & Prose 1956–1985.*

Foye's *Selected Poems* for the first time reprinted a large portion of *State Capitol*, overcoming Wieners's view that the book was a "a single work—a single *poem*," never to "be excerpted in any form," in the service of affirming its culminating status within Wieners's oeuvre. Although Black Sparrow Press reproduced this set of poems in a new typesetting that struggled to convey the book's emphasis on the visual page, Foye deserves great credit for this retransmission of *State Capitol* to future readers. "We didn't really have, in those days, the perspective on things that we have today," Foye recalled in 2018 of his decision to so prominently feature late work in *Selected Poems*, including the 1984 series titled *She'd Turn on a Dime*.

> There was still a stigma attached to this work; there was still a very strong opposition between rationality and irrationality. A lot of John's friends, the old guard, thought that he'd completely lost it and this was just, you know, a madman and that Shively and company were doing him a great disservice. And I was coming to grips with this work as well. But the thing that kept drawing me back was how good it was. The writing was so vivid, and the imagery brilliant, the flow from line to line. I thought they were great poems, and I remember finally one day thinking, "Well, he's still using language. And as long as he's using language, he's on his own grounds." That was my starting point. Slowly, reading them over, I came to really love them for what they were. Magnificent creations. And the consummation of the ambition of Olson's "Projective Verse."

Since all but "a few hundred" copies of the Good Gay Poets' remaining inventory of *State Capitol*, as well as the negatives, were destroyed in a fire set to *Fag Rag*'s offices by arsonists in 1982, Foye's *Selected Poems* was the standard reference where three decades of readers (including this one) first discovered Wieners's tour de force. Around the turn of the millennium, there emerged a deepening critical reckoning with the book, which continues to the present, manifested by writers including Geoff Ward, John Wilkinson, Andrea Brady, John Temple, and Cedar Sigo. In 2015, *Supplication: Selected Poems of John Wieners*, edited by Joshua Beckman, CAConrad, and myself, continued to keep

State Capitol in circulation, presenting thirty-eight pages from the Good Gay Poets' edition in a full-scale facsimile laid out by Wave Books designer Jeff Clark ("Quemadura").

"In the history of art," the philosopher Theodor W. Adorno wrote, "late works are the catastrophes." *State Capitol* is difficult by design, and fits this theme of mature masterpieces that don't "surrender themselves to mere delectation." In his essays on the project, Shively asserts that *State Capitol* was meant to be "a weapon of survival," anathema to "the poetry establishment," an always "unassimilable voice and presence." Writing in 1987 of the fire five years earlier at *Fag Rag*'s offices, he calls this "the definitive exegesis of *Behind the State Capitol*." A hyperbole, but there's something to it; I'm reminded of how the poet Francesca Lisette once remarked to me that so many Wieners poems end in flames ("I burn in the memory of love," etc.). According to Shively, Wieners intended *State Capitol* to be the first book of a trilogy like the *Divine Comedy*, with planned sequels titled *Under Bismark Bridges* and *Marble Harbor*. Wieners had written most of part two, but he "threw it away and abandoned the whole project" when the world failed to understand his *Inferno*. Nevertheless, *State Capitol* has smoldered through the years, singed but not snuffed, retaining all the heat of 1975's liberatory aspirations, intensities, affects. With this 50th anniversary edition, the torch is passed so that it may continue to light the way forward.

—Robert Dewhurst
Altadena, CA

SELECTED BIBLIOGRAPHY

Bronski, Michael. "The Last Gay Liberationist." *Boston Review*, December 20, 2017. https://www.bostonreview.net/articles/michael-bronski-last-gay-liberationist/.

Butterick, George F. "Wieners, John (Joseph)." In *Contemporary Poets*, 3rd ed., edited by James Vinson, 1652–54. St. Martin's, 1980.

Damon, Maria. "John Wieners in the Matrix of Massachusetts Institutions: A Psychopoeticgeography." *Journal of Beat Studies* 3 (2014): 69–92.

Dewhurst, Robert. "*Gay Sunshine*, Pornopoetic Collage, and Queer Archive." In *Porn Archives*, edited by Tim Dean, Steven Ruszczycky, and David Squires, 213–33. Duke University Press, 2014.

Dunn, James C. "The Mesmerizing Apparition of the Oracle of Joy Street: A Critical Study of John Wieners' Life and Later Work in Boston." MA thesis, Harvard Extension School, 2017.

Fredman, Stephen. *Contextual Practice: Assemblage and the Erotic in Postwar Poetry and Art*. Stanford University Press, 2010.

Grundy, David. "'A Gay Presence': John Wieners, Charley Shively, and *Fag Rag*." In *Never by Itself Alone: Queer Poetry, Queer Communities in Boston and the Bay Area, 1944–Present*, 157–77. Oxford University Press, 2024.

Mitzel, John. "[Story of *Fag Rag*] Part 2." December 17, 2012. Video, 11 min., 16 sec. https://vimeo.com/56042143.

Raha, Nat. "Queer Labour in Boston: The Work of John Wieners, Gay Liberation and *Fag Rag*." In *Poetry and Work: Work in Modern and Contemporary Anglophone Poetry*, edited by Jo Lindsay Walton and Ed Luker, 195–243. Palgrave Macmillan, 2019.

Shively, Charley. "*Fag Rag*: The Most Loathsome Publication in the English Language." In *Insider Histories of the Vietnam Era Underground Press, Part 2*, edited by Ken Wachsberger, 97–120. Michigan State University Press, 2012.

———. "Johnjob: Editing *Behind the State Capitol or Cincinnati Pike*." In "Homage to Wieners," edited by Kevin Killian, special issue, *Mirage*, no. 1 (1985): 78–83.

———. "Sequins & Switchblades: In Extremis Exegesis; A Reading of John Wieners' *Selected Poems: 1958–1984*." *Fag Rag*, no. 44 (1987): 28–33.

———. "What Happened to the Mind of John Wieners?" *Gay Sunshine*, no. 26/27 (Winter 1975–76): 32–33.

Sullivan, Hannah. *The Work of Revision*. Harvard University Press, 2013.

Wieners, John. Interview by Charles Shively, February 8, 1973. *Gay Sunshine*, no. 17 (March–April 1973): 1–3.

———. *Yours Presently: The Selected Letters of John Wieners*. Edited by Michael Seth Stewart. University of New Mexico Press, 2020.

Wieners, John, and Charles Shively. *I Watch You All Morning Long with My Hand over My Mouth: The Letters of John Wieners & Charles Shively; 1969–1975*. Edited by Michael Seth Stewart. Published by the editor, 2016.

And interviews of Alan Davies, Raymond Foye, John Mitzel, and Charles Shively, conducted by the author between 2011 and 2018.

ACKNOWLEDGMENTS

Robert Dewhurst would like to thank Dorothea Lasky, Alison Fraser and others at the Poetry Collection (University of Buffalo Libraries), and Michael Seth Stewart, for their support with secondary sources; and Stephen Coles and Kevin Thompson, of the online forum Font ID, for their help identifying vintage typefaces.

The publishers wish to thank the Beinecke Rare Book & Manuscript Library at Yale University, Charley Shively Papers (Timothy Young, Curator of Rare Books and Manuscripts); Michael Bronski, Professor of the Practice in Activism and Media, Studies of Women, Gender and Sexuality, Harvard University; Isla C. Davis, Woodberry Poetry Room, Lamont Library, Harvard University; The History Project, Boston; and all of the brave members of the Fag Rag/Good Gay Poets collective, living and dead.

OTHER TITLES FROM THE SONG CAVE:

1. *A Dark Dreambox of Another Kind* by **Alfred Starr Hamilton**
2. *My Enemies* by **Jane Gregory**
3. *Rude Woods* by **Nate Klug**
4. *Georges Braque and Others* by **Trevor Winkfield**
5. *The Living Method* by **Sara Nicholson**
6. *Splash State* by **Todd Colby**
7. *Essay Stanzas* by **Thomas Meyer**
8. *Illustrated Games of Patience* by **Ben Estes**
9. *Dark Green* by **Emily Hunt**
10. *Honest James* by **Christian Schlegel**
11. *M* by **Hannah Brooks-Motl**
12. *What the Lyric Is* by **Sara Nicholson**
13. *The Hermit* by **Lucy Ives**
14. *The Orchid Stories* by **Kenward Elmslie**
15. *Do Not Be a Gentleman When You Say Goodnight* by **Mitch Sisskind**
16. *HAIRDO* by **Rachel B. Glaser**
17. *Motor Maids across the Continent* by **Ron Padgett**
18. *Songs for Schizoid Siblings* by **Lionel Ziprin**
19. *Professionals of Hope: The Selected Writings of* **Subcomandante Marcos**
20. *Fort Not* by **Emily Skillings**
21. *Riddles, Etc.* by **Geoffrey Hilsabeck**
22. *CHARAS: The Improbable Dome Builders* by **Syeus Mottel** (Co-published with Pioneer Works)
23. *YEAH NO* by **Jane Gregory**
24. *Nioque of the Early-Spring* by **Francis Ponge**
25. *Smudgy and Lossy* by **John Myers**
26. *The Desert* by **Brandon Shimoda**
27. *Scardanelli* by **Friederike Mayröcker**
28. *The Alley of Fireflies and Other Stories* by **Raymond Roussel**
29. *CHANGES: Notes on Choreography* by **Merce Cunningham** (Co-published with the Merce Cunningham Trust)
30. *My Mother Laughs* by **Chantal Akerman**
31. *Earth* by **Hannah Brooks-Motl**
32. *Everything and Other Poems* by **Charles North**
33. *Paper Bells* by **Phan Nhiên Hạo**

34. *Photographs: Together & Alone* by **Karlheinz Weinberger**

35. *A Better Place Is Hard to Find* by **Aaron Fagan**

36. *Rough Song* by **Blanca Varela**

37. *In the Same Light: 200 Poems for Our Century From the Migrants & Exiles of the Tang Dynasty,* translated by **Wong May**

38. *On the Mesa: An Anthology of Bolinas Writing (50th Anniversary Edition),* edited by **Ben Estes and Joel Weishaus**

39. *Listen My Friend, This Is the Dream I Dreamed Last Night* by **Cody-Rose Clevidence**

40. *Poetries* by **Georges Schehadé**

41. *Wings in Time* by **Callie Garnett**

42. *Two Murals* by **Jesús Castillo**

43. *Punks: New & Selected Poems* by **John Keene**

44. *ABC Moonlight* by **Ben Estes**

45. *Star Lake* by **Arda Collins**

46. *The Maybe-Bird* by **Jennifer Elise Foerster**

47. *Seriously Well* by **Helge Torvund**

48. *Dereliction* by **Gabrielle Octavia Rucker**

49. *Bookworm: Conversations with* **Michael Silverblatt**

50. *April* by **Sara Nicholson**

51. *Valley of the Many-Colored Grasses* by **Ronald Johnson**

52. *The Sphinx and the Milky Way: Selections from the Notebooks of* **Charles Burchfield**

53. *Telling the Truth as It Comes Up: Selected Talks & Essays 1991–2018* by **Alice Notley**

54. *Lunar Solo: Selected Poems* by **Jules Laforgue**

55. *Stranger* by **Emily Hunt**

56. *The Selkie* by **Morgan Võ**

57. *Hereafter* by **Alan Felsenthal**

58. *Cold Dogs* by **Zan de Parry**

59. *Saturday* by **Margaret Ross**

60. *Many Poems* by **Roberta Iannamico**

61. *Ultraviolet of the Genuine* by **Hannah Brooks-Motl**

62. *Silkworm's Pansori* by **David Seung**

63. *Tantrums in Air* by **Emily Skillings**

64. *Jump Cuts: Essays on Surrealism, Film, Music, Culture, and Other Utopian Topics* by **Mark Polizzotti**

65. *Earthly: Selected Poems* by **Jean Follain**

66. *Nebraska* by **George Whitmore**

The Song Cave
www.the-song-cave.com

Cover photo: John Wieners, Boston State Capitol, 1983. Photo by Raymond Foye
Frontispiece photo: John Wieners on his fire escape, 44 Joy Street, Apt. 10,
Boston, 1972. Photo by Judith Harwood

ISBN: 979-8-9912988-7-2
Library of Congress Cataloguing-in-Publication Data has been applied for.

FIRST PRINTING

This volume is a facsimile edition of the original 1975 publication.